Expert Systems
Concepts and Examples

J L Alty and M J Coombs

PUBLISHED BY NCC PUBLICATIONS

British Library Cataloguing in Publication Data

Alty, J.L.
   Expert systems – concepts and examples.
   I. Title   II. Coombs, M.J.
   001.64   QA76.9.E96
   ISBN 0-85012-399-2

First published in 1984 by:

NCC Publications, The National Computing Centre Ltd, Oxford Road, Manchester M1 7ED, England.

Typeset in 10pt Times Roman by UPS Blackburn Ltd, 76-80 Northgate, Blackburn, Lancashire, and printed by Hobbs the Printers of Southampton.

ISBN 0-85012-399-2

Preface

This book is intended to fill a gap in the current tutorial literature on expert systems. Most currently available texts are aimed at the academic market-place and usually consist of collections of papers detailing current interest in narrow research areas. Whilst such texts are most valuable for the research worker already versed in the field, they usually do not provide a reasonably comprehensive introduction to the subject for those with a defined application need but without the requisite skills in Artificial Intelligence and associated research areas.

This book is therefore aimed at the computing professional (or student in information technology) who requires a sufficiently detailed overview to enable him to conduct an intelligent appraisal of the relevance of the subject without being sidetracked by particular research issues. The style adopted is deliberately non-academic in that we have not referenced work in the text itself in order to ensure a sequentially developed, uninterrupted argument involving the principal concepts in the field, and their application. At the end of the book we provide an extensive reference list to enable readers to further explore issues of interest. Following the title, the book is divided into two parts: Part I – Background Concepts; and Part II – Examples of Expert Systems.

Part I examines the fundamental aspects of representation and control which are germane to the development of expert systems. Chapter 1 is intended to provide a bridge to the more formal treatments in Chapters 2 and 3. It treats the issues of representation and control in an informal way using examples from traditional data processing, and outlines, via predicate calculus and production systems, possible approaches to the problems raised. Chapter 2 examines the attempts to formalise inference. Although some knowledge of formal logic would be useful here, we hope that the reader who has not met logic before will be able to grasp the essentials. The chapter highlights the impasse reached in the development of automated inference systems which led many research workers to attack the problem using domain-dependent control structures. Chapter 3 outlines some useful representational techniques such as frames and semantic networks and provides the reader who is not familiar with LISP with at least a flavour of the language.

Part II opens with Chapter 4 in which we attempt to classify current expert systems according to their underlying control structure or knowledge base. This classification serves to place the four succeeding chapters in perspective. In Chapter 5 we deal with systems which use uncertain evidence in their reasoning – MYCIN and PROSPECTOR. The chapter highlights the usefulness of production systems and their utility in providing explanation facilities. Chapter 6 covers INTERNIST and CASNET. The former illustrates a non-production system approach based on set-theoretic concepts, the latter exploits causal knowledge.

Chapter 7 takes the DENDRALs (Heuristic and Meta) as its subjects. These were amongst the earliest examples of successful expert systems and are still being used and extended. Both systems work with a very large search space progressively pruning it using a plan-generate-test approach. The early success of the DENDRAL systems inspired the development of the whole area of expert systems in Artificial Intelligence. Chapter 8 discusses the application of the technique of abstraction using R1 and MOLGEN as examples. R1 is a system which is now in everyday use with a large computer manufacturer and is used for configuring computer systems. MOLGEN is concerned with design of experiments in molecular genetics.

In Chapter 9 we return to the problems posed in Chapter 2 concerning the automation of logical inference. Using Skolem functions, clausal form and resolution techniques we show how a solution can be found and, in particular, how the language PROLOG was developed. The chapter concludes with a brief discussion of existing issues in expert system research.

We have tried to condense the knowledge and expertise of expert systems into a tightly constructed and concise treatise which of itself contains the essence of expert system methodology and its application to real problems. The task has not been an easy one and we hope that those who feel we should have given a more lengthy treatment to certain issues will recognise the competing constraints of conciseness and comprehensibility.

Acknowledgements

Various organisations have given permission to reproduce published diagrammatic material. We are grateful to:

Alfred Publishing Company Incorporated, California (permission for Figure 3.14);

Carnegie-Mellon University Department of Computer Science, Pennsylvania (Figures 8.1 to 8.3);

Edinburgh University Press (Figure 7.1);

North-Holland Publishing Company, Amsterdam (Figures 6.4 and 6.5);

SRI International, California (Figures 5.5 to 5.9);

Stanford University Heuristic Programming Project, California (Figures 5.3 and 8.4 to 8.11).

We also wish to express our thanks to Jeanette Walsh for meticulously typing the manuscript and to Sheila Hughes for carefully checking it. Any mistakes which remain, however, are ours.

J L Alty
M J Coombs
University of Strathclyde
Glasgow, 1983

Contents

Page

Preface

Acknowledgements

PART I   BACKGROUND CONCEPTS   15

1   Traditional Data Processing and Expert Systems   17

    1.1   Introduction   17
    1.2   The Representation Problem   17
    1.3   Knowledge Representation   19
    1.4   The Traditional Approach   23
    1.5   An Alternative Representation for Classes,
          Relations and Rules   28
    1.6   An Alternative Control Structure – Production Systems   29
    1.7   Control Structures and Domain Dependence   31
    1.8   Other Limitations of the Traditional Approach   33
    1.9   The Way Ahead   36

2   Fundamentals of Predicate Calculus and Logical Inference   37

    2.1   Introduction   37
    2.2   Predicate Calculus and the Representation of Knowledge   39
    2.3   Logical Inference   43
    2.4   Problems with Predicate Calculus for Knowledge
          Processing   49

3 Computational Approaches to Representation and Control   53

   3.1   The Shift to Knowledge-Based Systems   53
   3.2   LISP – A Language for Programming
        Knowledge-Based Systems   57
   3.3   The Representation of Domain Knowledge   60
   3.4   Problems of Control   76

PART II EXAMPLES OF EXPERT SYSTEMS   83

4 Expert Systems and Expert Problem-Solvers   85

   4.1   Knowledge-Based Problem-Solving   85
   4.2   A Classification Scheme for Expert Systems   89

**5 The Handling of Uncertain Evidence – MYCIN
    and PROSPECTOR**   93

   5.1   Introduction   93
   5.2   MYCIN (EMYCIN) Overview   94
   5.3   PROSPECTOR Overview   103
   5.4   Conclusions   115

**6 Associative and Causal Approaches to Diagnosis –
    INTERNIST and CASNET**   119

   6.1   Introduction   119
   6.2   The INTERNIST Project   120
   6.3   CASNET   129

**7 Reducing Large Search Spaces Through Factoring –
    Heuristic DENDRAL and Meta-DENDRAL**   137

   7.1   Processing Large Search Spaces   137
   7.2   The Application Task   138
   7.3   Heuristic DENDRAL   142
   7.4   Meta-DENDRAL   146

**8 Handling Large Search Spaces Through the Use
    of Abstraction – R1 and MOLGEN**   153

   8.1   Levels of Description in a Search Space   153
   8.2   R1   155

8.3   R1 Conclusions   161
8.4   MOLGEN   161
8.5   MOLGEN Conclusions   175

9   Further Developments in Expert Systems   177

9.1   The Automation of Predicate Logic   177
9.2   Some Advantages of Predicate Logic   189
9.3   Developments in Expert Systems   191

Bibliography   195

Index   201

Part I

Background Concepts

1 Traditional Data Processing and Expert Systems

1.1 INTRODUCTION

Expert Systems have their origins in traditional data processing. They are the result of continuous attempts to improve and extend the automation of some aspects of human information processing. In order to accomplish this task we need to represent in a computer system the nature of the data and processes involved.

1.2 THE REPRESENTATION PROBLEM

A digital computer transforms an input sequence of symbols into an output sequence. The available primitive transformations are very limited and are defined in its electronics. If we regard the symbol sequences as representing binary numbers, primitive transformations will amongst other things add two sequences together, subtract them, shift the patterns to the right or the left, and compare two sequences to see if they are identical.

The computer has no knowledge of what it is doing. It mimics operations which we understand in the real world. The word "mimic" is used deliberately. Anyone familiar with computer arithmetic will realise that it is only an approximation to real-world arithmetic. Design considerations for example require sequences to be stored in fixed length units (often called words). Such boundaries do not exist in the real world and the transformation of sequences which are longer than the word boundaries can lead to unexpected results.

The primitive transformations are only valid if the input sequences are presented in the proper format and the output sequences are interpreted correctly. Both these activities are human activities. The problem is essentially one of *representation*. We must define a valid formalism for presenting sequences of symbols to the computer which unambiguously represent what we intend, and we must define the primitive transformations (usually in electronics) such that the transformations carried out on the symbols by the computer have an unambiguous meaning to us. Having achieved this we are then able to understand the sequence of output symbols. Furthermore, we have to define a representation which enables us to inform the computer of the correct set of transformations required (ie the program). The program is simply a sequence composed from the set of primitive operations which mimic some real-world information processing activity which we understand and which we would otherwise have had to carry out in our heads. Thus in constructing a computer program we are automating a part of our knowledge processing.

Once the primitive operations have been defined we can then select sequences of these operations to represent higher-level operations. For example, a sequence of addition or subtraction primitives can represent the multiplication or division of two numbers. This synthesising process can be continued to provide yet higher-level functions such as square roots, exponentiation, trigonometrical functions, etc. Finally we can define sets of symbol sequences which enable us to program in higher-level languages and in which we define meaningful and useful constructions to assist us in representing that part of the knowledge processing which we wish to automate.

We can also define alternative interpretations for our sequences. Codes can be devised which allow us to represent alphabetic characters as special symbols and, by choosing these codes so that the bit patterns of succeeding letters of the alphabet have an ascending numerical interpretation, we can capture the essence of alphabetic sequencing in our representation. Other higher level functions can then be defined which can manipulate strings of characters, eg concatenation, comparing strings for equality, alphabetic sequencing, or selection of parts of sequences.

Traditional data processing therefore is made possible by the definition of appropriate representations, both for the data we wish to manipulate and for the sequence of operations which we wish to perform. It is important to realise that the choice of representation is crucial. It defines ultimately what types of knowledge processing can or cannot be automated. As traditional data processing has developed, inadequacies in our representation schemes have become apparent. The recent intense activity in defining Data Base Management Systems is a response to inadequacies in the ways in which we represent data in secondary storage. Data base systems are an attempt to define a higher level representation of the logical connections between data. The relational and network approaches are simply different attempts at solving these problems.

Many other problems associated with our traditional representational techniques (and hence the programming languages we use) are now beginning to become apparent as we try to automate more and more of human reasoning. The knowledge processing of a human expert, for example, draws upon large banks of information, some of which may be incomplete and which can be presented in many different forms. The processing by which an expert sifts, synthesises and transforms the initial data is poorly understood. If we wish to automate such reasoning we will need to represent the essential characteristics of the way in which the expert approaches and solves a problem. The traditional representation techniques are simply inadequate to cope with such problems and we are in danger of reaching an impasse imposed upon us by our representational limitations. Fortunately workers in Artificial Intelligence have been examining the representation problem for a number of years. In this chapter we examine anew the knowledge representation problem and introduce informally some new approaches derived from Artificial Intelligence research.

1.3   KNOWLEDGE REPRESENTATION

Human beings have "knowledge" about the world in which they live. Some of this knowledge is fairly generally known and shared by most people, such as that required to drive a car or eat a meal. Other knowledge is more specialised, such as that we normally ascribe to experts. Whatever its nature, however, knowledge can usually be represented in terms of facts about the world (ie classifications of and relationships between objects), procedures or rules for manipulating facts, and information about when or how to apply the rules or procedures.

We normally group objects by organising them into classes. Peter, John, Ann and Fred can be thought of as objects. They can be assigned to the class "person". Additionally Peter, John and Fred would be classified as "male" and Ann as "female". One obvious advantage of classification is that it eases memory load since we only need to know the characteristics of a class rather than each individual object. We can also define relationships between classes (or individual objects). Thus we can define the relation "manages (A,B)" to mean that B is managed by A. Examples of such a relationship might be

> manages (peter,john)
> manages (john,ann)
> manages (ann,fred)

implying a reporting structure (another relationship) of Peter-John-Ann-Fred. The above relationship is an example of a relation between like objects, but one can equally well define relationships between different objects (eg "owns (peter,car)"). Knowledge about objects and their relationships enables us to classify and relate them one to another.

The second type of knowledge – rules – enables us to specify how to infer new instances of a class, or new instances of a relation, from hitherto unclassified objects. For example, if we define the relation "reports-to (B,A)" to mean that B reports to A (perhaps via other managers) then we can state the rule that

> reports-to (C,A) is TRUE
>   IF EITHER manages (A,C) is TRUE
>   OR manages (A,B) AND manages (B,C) are TRUE

This is a rather limited rule. It only applies to first- or second-level reporting, but within this constraint it does enable us to generate new instances of the "reports-to" relation which we may not have previously known. For example, the rule would enable us to deduce that "reports-to (ann,peter)" and "reports-to (fred,john)" are TRUE. Because of the simple two-level definition of the above rule it cannot, for example, be used to infer that "reports-to (fred,peter)" is TRUE. To do this we need a more powerful rule involving recursion

> reports-to (C,A) is TRUE
>   IF EITHER manages (A,C) is TRUE
>   OR manages (A,B) is TRUE
>   AND reports-to (C,B) is TRUE

The first part of this recursive rule deals with direct reporting, the second with indirect reporting.

If we ask the question "reports-to (john,peter)?" then the first "IF" part of the rule is immediately true so that the question is answered

TRUE. If we ask the question "reports-to (fred,peter)?" the processing is more complex. Table 1.1 below shows the processing involved in the application of the above rule.

Column 1 indicates the initial question. Column 2 details the evaluation of the EITHER part of the rule. Column 3 details the evaluation of the OR part of the rule which only takes place if the EITHER part fails. The evaluation of the OR part always results in a subsequent query, which then becomes a new question to be answered.

Note the recursive processing with "reports-to". This is quite a complex procedure yet the rule itself is quite simple and understandable. In computing terms a rule is essentially a one-line procedure.

Of course the representation of some knowledge processing will require a very complex set of rules, and experts will tend to use rules or procedures which non-experts will not understand. Often an expert himself may not really understand the processes he actually carries out in making a judgement.

So far we have introduced two components – facts and rules. The third requirement for knowledge processing is a control structure; this determines the way in which the various rules are applied. Essentially a control

Question	EITHER part	OR part	New Question
reports-to (fred,peter)?	manages (peter,fred)? false	manages (peter,B)? true B = john	reports-to (fred,john)?
reports-to (fred,john)?	manages (john,fred)? false	manages (john,B)? true B = ann	reports-to (fred,ann)?
reports-to (fred,ann)?	manages (ann,fred) true		

Therefore   reports-to (fred,ann) is TRUE
So   reports-to (fred,john) is TRUE
So   reports-to (fred,peter) is TRUE which answers the question

Table 1.1   Reports-to Example

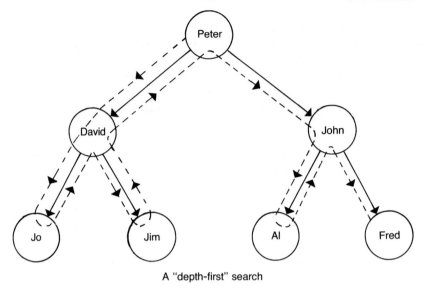

A "depth-first" search

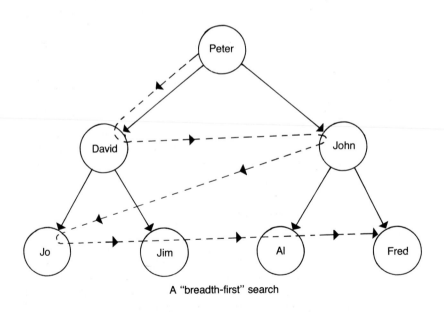

A "breadth-first" search

Figure 1.1   Processing a Hierarchy

structure enables a decision to be taken on what rule to apply next. In most real situations the number of rules required will be very large and many different forms of control structure are possible. Rules could be taken in sequence, or some subset of rules might be required to decide which other rules to apply (these can be thought of as higher level, or meta-rules). The mechanism by which a rule is applied in situations in which there is a choice is also a control structure problem. For example, when we considered the processing of the rule in Table 1.1, there was only one possible path to be followed in answering the question. Normally however a management hierarchy has a variety of paths, as illustrated in Figure 1.1.

At certain points we are faced with a choice and we need to have a consistent method defined by the control structure for selecting paths. Obviously any consistent approach will do (approaches to this problem are discussed in some detail in Chapter 3), but one obvious way of solving the problem would be to always follow the left-most branch of a tree first until either the query was solved or the end of the branch reached. In the latter case we would then "backtrack" to the last choice point and examine the alternative branches in the same way. Thus in Figure 1.1. the processing of the query "reports-to (fred,peter)?" would follow the dotted line. This is called a "depth-first" search. A "breadth-first" search is also shown.

To describe knowledge processing therefore we can utilise declarative knowledge (classes and relations) and procedural knowledge (rules and control structures). The boundary between the two is very flexible. Generally, the less knowledge we declare, the more procedural knowledge is required and vice versa. In reality the distinction between declarative and procedural knowledge is not very meaningful since the definition of a rule could be regarded as declarative.

1.4   THE TRADITIONAL APPROACH

1.4.1   Classifications and Relations

The writing of a computer program involves a decision about the position of the boundary between computer and human knowledge processing. In reality the boundary usually shifts as we write. Often, it is realised that a program can provide more useful information than originally intended or, conversely, some aspects of the problem prove to be too difficult to define in computer terms.

The first task involves the classification of all objects which are to be manipulated by the computer. This classification in reality is the construction of a one-to-one relationship between computing symbols and external objects or ideas.

Classification of sets of similar objects is usually achieved by providing a label (or variable name) and an index. The label defines the class and the index defines an occurrence, or instance, of the class. The conventional array is useful in this respect. An array (in BASIC) NAME$ (I) identifies the class of objects "Name" (say) and the possible values of I define instances of actual names. In COBOL or PASCAL more sophisticated structures can be used, but the idea is the same. Another technique used for classification is the field position in a file record. The Employee No., say, could be defined to be the third field in the record. This is the class label. Different instances of Employee No. occur in different records, thus the record number together with the field definition defines an instance of this class.

In conventional systems we are usually required to provide additional classifications in order to clarify to the computer the nature of the processing required. For example, in BASIC the $ at the end of the variable name indicates that the variable should be treated as a string of characters not a number. We would also need to define NAME$ as an array and indicate the maximum value of the index. Finally we would need to define the nature of the index, in this case an integer. Thus to classify a series of names in BASIC we need to:

a)   define the field as text;
b)   define the array;
c)   define the maximum index;
d)   define the nature of the index.

Most other conventional languages require the computational nature of a variable to be defined, for example in the DATA DIVISION in COBOL, or type definition in PASCAL.

Notice that classification involves the creation of a number of "dummy" variables which have properties of their own. For example, there is an implied ordering for the index which may, or may not, have any relevance to the problem domain. In many systems the maximum size of the array causes difficulties and a large number is usually chosen to encompass all possibilities.

Relationships define connections between objects we have already classified. In conventional languages we do this by assigning another set of symbols to the relationship which we then interpret (or classify it in terms of other relations). A rather similar approach to that used for classification is adopted – a label and an index are used. Once again, the label defines the relation and the index an instance of it. The similarity to classification is not surprising since in fact we are merely classifying relationships. The situation is, however, more complex because we have to relate existing classes and there may be many in one relation.

Arrays or structures are normally used within programs to define relationships. For example, we might wish to establish the relationship between a student and his marks in particular subjects. An array could be defined MARK (I, J) which contains the mark for student I in subject J. There is, in fact, a double relation here; a student and his marks, or a subject and the relevant marks. If the index I defines instances of the former relationship, then J defines members of the relation for that instance. The roles of I and J can be reversed to provide the other relationship. Note again that we have created new dummy variables with their own implied orderings and maxima in order to define the relationship. Similar techniques would be used in COBOL or PASCAL. However, the capability in these languages of defining structures containing different data types makes relation definition much easier and avoids the use of a member index. An index is still required to define instances of the relation (eg use of OCCURS in COBOL).

Similarly, position may be used to define a relationship. The commonest example is a file. A record is really a definition of a relationship between the fixed fields within it. The position within the record defines the various classes taking part in the relationship and the record number defines instances of the relation. Thus a record serves to classify and to signify a relationship. The student/marks relationship above might equally well be represented by a series of records, one for each student, containing the marks for each subject in fixed fields. Note, however, that in this representation it requires considerable effort to examine the subject/marks relationship. This is a clear example of how representation affects processing.

1.4.2   Procedures

Procedures create new instances of relationships and classes from existing ones. Figure 1.2 below illustrates a PASCAL procedure for calculating new instances of the class SALARY.

```
FOR I := 1 TO IMAX DO
BEGIN
    SALARY [I] := RATE [I] * HOURS [I];
    WRITELN (NAMES [I], " ", SALARY [I])
END;
```

Figure 1.2   SALARY Instantiation Procedure

The procedure operates on existing classes of RATE (the rate the individual I works at), HOURS (the no. of hours I worked) and refers to his name (NAME is the text of I's name). It produces new instances of SALARY. Incidentally it also adds information to the relation NAME–HOURS–RATE–SALARY which exists implicitly because of I.

Note first that the operation of the procedure depends upon previous classifications. It also needs a value for the dummy variable IMAX which in this instance does have a correspondence with the outside world – the total number of employees. Note also that the computer cannot create new classes or relationships. These are all defined during the writing of the program. It can only instantiate existing classes or relationships.

Figure 1.3 below illustrates a procedure for creating instances of a wealth class called RICH. Each employee in RICH earns over $100 per hour.

Stripped of all its additional computing knowledge this rule can be rewritten in a much more understandable form

rich (X) is TRUE IF rate (X) > 100

It is important to note the influence of our classification and relation definitions upon the procedure constructions. Because we have created additional indices to define classes and relationships we need iterative constructions to manipulate them. This results in artificial constructs such

```
J := 0;
FOR I := 1 TO IMAX DO
BEGIN
    IF RATE [I] > 100 THEN
    BEGIN
    J := J + 1;
    RICH [J] := NAME [I]
    END
END;
```

Figure 1.3   Instantiation of a Class

as DO . . . WHILE, FOR . . . DO, REPEAT . . . UNTIL, etc, which iterate on these dummy variables. Note also that such constructs tend to obscure the meaning of what is going on.

1.4.3   Conventional Control Structures

Given a set of classes, relationships between them, and some procedures, how do we arrive at a desired result? The control structure determines in what sequence the various procedures are applied. In conventional systems the simplicity of the control structure has caused serious problems and it is one reason for the development of structured programming techniques. Essentially, the control structure is "if the next step is not explicitly defined by a language construct, execute the next instruction". Conventional programs therefore tend to have a large sequential element, punctuated by iterative procedures (often containing nested iterative procedures) and perhaps some frowned-upon GOTOs. These programs are difficult to understand because extra knowledge is embedded in them which is additional to the problem domain – knowledge concerning the reforming of the problem into the computer domain. The rule we derived from Figure 1.3 illustrates this point strikingly, being a declarative or non-procedural representation of the procedure in Figure 1.3.

The conventional approach typifies program-driven processing. What happens next is predetermined by the program at any particular point.

We see this philosophy even carried over into real-time programming when the external environment can asynchronously "interrupt" the program at any point. On receipt of an interrupt the current situation is saved, and an interrupt routine loaded and executed. On termination of this routine the saved situation is retrieved and processing carries on as before. Thus even interrupt handling is essentially program driven. It is interesting to note that human beings often do not work in this way. If interrupted, we deal with the interruption but sometimes forget the previous situation and may never return to it unless reminded to do so by another external interrupt. A short observation of a conversation between two human beings will emphasise this point. Human beings are usually data-driven, and this is often a very efficient way of dealing with many situations, particularly in uncertain environments.

1.4.4 Conclusion

We have shown how knowledge and processing procedures are represented in conventional systems. The representation is cumbersome, involving the definition of additional information concerned with computational mechanisms which do not exist in the original problem. The control structure is simple but this is only because a number of constructs have to be defined to manipulate the classes and relations we have defined. The representation is too closely connected with the way in which a computer operates.

1.5 AN ALTERNATIVE REPRESENTATION FOR CLASSES, RELATIONS AND RULES

An alternative approach to representing classes and relations can be achieved through the use of a predicate calculus notation. This will be discussed in more detail in Chapter 2, but in essence we define relationships between different objects by a relation name (called a predicate), followed by a list of the objects related in this way enclosed in parentheses.

For example, the fact that "John likes Joan" can be represented as

         likes (john,joan)
or   likes (joan,john)

The interpretation of the order of the arguments is left to the programmer. If Peter, Fred and Jo are employees, we could represent this as employees (peter,jo,fred)

where the order is immaterial. This of course is a relationship which classifies.

The notation achieves further expressive power by using variables as arguments (usually depicted with a starting capital letter), and the connectives such as AND, OR, NOT and IF . . . THEN . . . . For example, the following rule uses variables and connectives to define a general relationship between "reports-to" and "manages".

> reports-to (C,A) IF manages (A,C) OR
> (manages (A,B) AND
> reports-to (C,B))

This should be interpreted as "reports-to (C,A) is TRUE if either manages (A,C) is TRUE or manages (A,B) and reports-to (C,B) are both TRUE". Strictly speaking the scope of the variables for which the rule is true should be defined. In this case we assume that the rule is true for all instantiations.

Notice that there is no computer-specific knowledge in these definitions and that the rules are defined in the same notation as the classes and the relationships. In fact rules are relationships in which the set of clauses in the THEN part are implied by those in the IF part.

1.6   AN ALTERNATIVE CONTROL STRUCTURE – PRODUCTION SYSTEMS

What control structures could we adopt? One possibility is the production system. A production system consists of the three elements we have already defined – classifications and relationships, rules, and a control structure. The classifications and relations are termed the "data base" which essentially holds the declarative knowledge. The procedures are a set of rules of the type

> IF (condition) THEN (action)

and the control structure determines what rule is tried next. It is often called a rule interpreter. The (condition) is a test of the current state of the data base and the (action) updates the data base in some way.

Figure 1.4 illustrates a simple example which determines the largest and smallest of a set of numbers, where the data base contains the numbers A(1) to A(10), and NUMA contains the number of elements to be considered. MAX and MIN are fixed and assist us in ordering the numbers. TRY holds the current value of the trial number.

A rule "fires" when the IF condition is satisfied. Rules 2 and 3 update the data base with new values of MAX or MIN. Rule 4 updates TRY unconditionally when Rules 1, 2 and 3 can't fire. Eventually Rule 1 will fire and terminate processing. The control structure searches for a rule which fires. It then begins its search of the top again. Note that in this case the rules are order dependent. Figure 1.5 illustrates a production system in which the rules are order-independent.

It can be seen that the rules can be placed in any order. Provided we define our rules carefully, new functions can be inserted in the program, by simply adding extra rules. Order-independent rule systems are not that easy to construct. The IF condition must be unique for each rule. If the number of rules is large these conditions become quite complex.

DATABASE (classes and relations)

A(1) 5 A(2) 7 ....A(10) 21

NUMA 10 MAX 0 MIN 100,000

TRY 1

RULES (procedures)

1. IF TRY > NUMA THEN WRITELN (MAX, MIN); STOP;

2. IF A(TRY) > MAX THEN MAX := A(TRY);

3. IF A(TRY) < MIN THEN MIN := A(TRY);

4. IF no other rule has fired THEN TRY := TRY + 1;

CONTROL STRUCTURE

Try rules in sequence, until one fires. Then go to top of list of rules and start again. Terminate when STOP is signalled.

Figure 1.4 A Simple Production System

DATABASE

A(1) 5 A(2) 7...................A(10) 21

NUMA 10 MAX 0 MIN 100,000

TRY 1

RULES

1. IF ((TRY ≤ NUMA) AND (A(TRY) > MAX))
    THEN MAX := A(TRY);

2. IF ((TRY ≤ NUMA) AND (A(TRY) < MIN))
    THEN MIN := A(TRY);

3. IF (TRY > NUMA) THEN WRITELN (MAX, MIN); STOP;

4. IF ((TRY ≤ NUMA) AND (A(TRY) < MAX) AND (A(TRY) > MIN))
    THEN TRY := TRY + 1;

CONTROL STRUCTURE

Try each rule in turn, until one fires. Then start at top again. Terminate when STOP is signalled.

Figure 1.5   Order-Independent Rule System

Many other control structures are possible in addition to the production rule approach, and research in Artificial Intelligence has resulted in the discovery of a number of different approaches. One issue of importance is the relationship between the control structure and the knowledge domain.

1.7 CONTROL STRUCTURES AND DOMAIN DEPENDENCE

In the examples we have just given, the control structure is domain-independent. In other words its modus operandum does not depend upon knowledge of the domain under investigation. Such control structures are simple and neat. They enable us to clearly separate application knowledge (ie the data base of facts and relations and the rules) from the control operation itself. In many real-world problems this is not easy to achieve and it may not be desirable.

One simple example of domain dependence concerns the effect of context. In many problems, sets of rules may only apply in certain circumstances or contexts. It is therefore convenient (and efficient) to group the sets of rules together by context and only allow a rule to be considered for firing if its appropriate context has been established. For example, if we wish to construct a knowledge-based program to determine the name of a living organism given some input data, there is little point in considering rules about fish if we have already established that the organism is land-based and has lungs.

In other problems, rules may have fixed and known relationships to each other. In such situations it may be convenient to cast the rules into a network as in Figure 1.6.

Such a network defines which rule will be checked for firing next. What we are actually doing is transferring some of the knowledge of the application from the declarative knowledge base to the control structure.

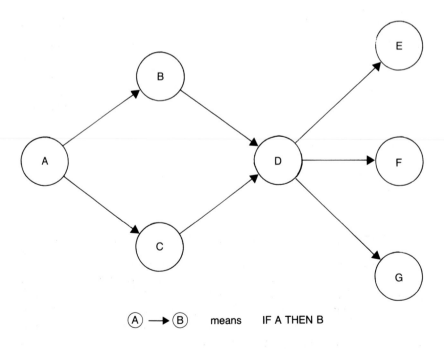

Figure 1.6   A Network of Rules

The drawback is, of course, that the control structure can now only be used in other knowledge processing situations which can be defined in a similar way. Domain dependence of the control structure is a very important concept and will become significant in later chapters.

1.8   OTHER LIMITATIONS OF THE TRADITIONAL APPROACH

There are other difficulties associated with traditional data processing which restrict us in defining the boundary between computer and human knowledge processing. The more important ones are inferred data, inexact reasoning, and problem solutions which cannot be written as conventional algorithms. All three are actually quite closely related.

1.8.1   Inferred Data

All programs infer new knowledge from old. The conventional approach moreover assumes that the order in which data is to be inferred is known. Thus the inference process can be cast into a conventional algorithm which sequentially builds up the inferred data and then further uses this inferred data to infer yet new data. Figure 1.2 gave an example of inferring SALARY data from RATE and HOURS data. In its present form it could not infer RATE data from SALARY and HOURS data. The whole process is carefully mapped out beforehand. In real situations it is often not clear, however, what will be given initially and what will need to be inferred.

Consider the problem of determining whether a relationship between two people exists, given some declarative knowledge about relationships. Assume we are given

> mother (mary,sue)
> sister (sue,joan)

where X (Y,Z) means "Y is the X of Z".

Clearly a human being can infer that "mother (mary,joan)" is TRUE.

If we increase the base of declarative data the situation rapidly becomes very complex. We will define further relationships (but keep to female-only relationships for simplicity)

> eg   mother (mary,sue)
> sister (sue,joan)

mother (joan,ellen)
sister (ellen,betty)

Not only can we infer "mother (mary,joan)" and "mother (joan,betty)" but we could infer other relationships such as "grandmother (mary,betty)", "auntie (sue,betty)" and "auntie (sue,ellen)", etc.

The essential point here is that the above data could be presented in many different ways, and yet the same total knowledge base could be derived. For example, we could have presented the initial data as:

mother (mary,joan)
auntie (sue,betty)
sister (betty,ellen)
mother (joan,ellen)
mother (mary,sue)

The conventional processing required to infer knowledge from this set would be different than in the former case. The only way in which a generalised algorithm can be constructed is to generate all possible relationships before answering any queries, but in a large declarative data base this would be a considerable waste of computer processing and would increase response time. The heart of the problem lies in the rigidity of the conventional control structure.

1.8.2 Inexact Reasoning

In the previous examples all of the knowledge was definite. The assertions were either TRUE or FALSE. In real life, however, knowledge tends to be "fuzzy". Nevertheless we are often able to infer things with reasonable certainty from inexact data. To do this, we must combine items of knowledge, together with their certainties, to infer new knowledge with a derived certainty.

We can add uncertainty to a class definition by simply adding, say, a certainty value between -1 and $+1$ (-1 meaning that it is FALSE and $+1$ meaning it is true)

eg   man (peter,1)
      man (hilary,0)

meaning that the name Peter is certainly of class "man" but Hilary can be a woman's name and therefore has only a 50% possibility of belonging to "man".

If we further know that

steelworker (hilary,1)

then we could increase the probability in the man relationship to, say, 90% because we could presume that steelworkers are generally of class "man". There are many ways of working out a combined probability but we might decide to take the average. Thus a rule of the form:

IF steelworker (X) AND man (X,p) THEN
CREATE man (X, (p + 1)/2)

This would not alter Peter's probability of being male were he a steelworker, but it would increase the probability of Hilary being male to 75%.

Once again, as with section 1.8.1 we may not be presented with the initial data in one possible form, so that a conventional system has difficulty in constructing a suitable algorithm. When the data base becomes large this would be very difficult to do. A rule approach can deal with the problem relatively easily. Some rules would be adjusting probabilities from the known information whilst others would take actions based upon probability levels.

1.8.3 Lack of Suitable Algorithms

This is really a generalisation of the problems already discussed in sections 1.8.1 and 1.8.2. In many situations it is not possible to construct an algorithm for solving a particular problem uniquely.

Conventional algorithms are not well suited to knowledge-based problem solving. For many real problems any algorithm which examined all possible problem states would have response times measured in years, yet human beings can solve such problems quickly and efficiently. The game of chess provides an excellent example of the difficulty. White has 20 possible opening moves to which Black can reply with a further 20. Thus White's second move can be made from 400 possible states. The combinational explosion as moves progress becomes rapidly unmanageable. The end game in particular emphasises the problem. With few pieces on the board, each player can have over 50 moves to choose from. Chess Masters do not operate by examining all possible states, rather they operate within short- and long-term strategies which are modified as the game progresses. Particular board situations induce the selection of a particular strategy from the large set available in their knowledge base. Another example is that afforded by "dry" stone-wall builders. The opening of the task is characterised by a large pile of different-sized stones. The expert wall builder does not know at the outset how and when he will select stones for the wall. Periodically he reviews the current state of the wall, the stones left, and selects an appropriate short-term strategy which may involve backtracking (taking stones off again). With an identical set of stones he may never actually ever build the same wall twice.

To solve such problems we need to choose from some set of strategies. We select from the set by examining the current state of the problem and use that strategy which will reduce the distance between the current state and the required solution. Little by little we approach the solution (or goal) by selecting strategies which we hope will bring us nearer to our goal.

1.9 THE WAY AHEAD

The previous sections have indicated that we need better ways of:

a) representing declarative knowledge such as classes and relationships without introducing computer-specific knowledge;

b) representing rules;

c) defining the control structure (dependent or independent of the knowledge domains).

If we succeed in these tasks we will be able to move the human/computer knowledge boundary in knowledge processing forward to encompass a wider range of information-processing activities. Our objective is to proceed beyond the traditional algorithmic approach so that we can automate a considerable part of the knowledge processing activities we normally ascribe to experts. The next chapter examines in a more formal way the problems we have discussed.

2 Fundamentals of Predicate Calculus and Logical Inference

2.1 INTRODUCTION

In preparation for later discussion of knowledge-based programs, we are now going to look more formally at the principles behind representation and control. Work in this area of relevance to expert systems has largely been conducted over the last 20 years within the discipline of Artificial Intelligence, a principal concern of which is the design of computer programs to undertake activities thought to require human intelligence. Programs have been developed, for example, to play chess or to identify badly machined engine components. However, the roots of the enterprise go back considerably further to one of the first academic disciplines – that of logic.

An important motivation for using computer programs is to increase the reliability with which knowledge is applied to a given information processing task. The problem of ensuring reliable information processing turns out to be a very old human concern, the earliest attempt to tackle it systematically being made by the Ancient Greeks. This was largely in response to the practical requirements of maintaining a democratic system of government within the city states, where action by public consent encouraged the study of both how to persuade in debate (honestly, or otherwise) and how to spot a false argument (or to put a true one). The former developed into the discipline of rhetoric and the latter into the discipline of logic.

Logic is thus critically concerned with the validity of arguments, ie with methods for determining whether given conclusions can be validly drawn from given assumed facts. Furthermore, it is of relevance to programming since a program is really a set of quasi-logical statements which are processed in some way to generate a conclusion. Within logic the notion of a "true argument" has a precise, clearly defined meaning; an argument is considered true if (and only if), when its assumptions are *all* true, its conclusions are also true.

In order to decide upon the acceptability of a particular argument, it is necessary to make some test. Within logic the method of doing this is to compare the text of interest against abstracted "patterns" of argument and to seek a match. Such patterns are termed "forms" and are made up of abstracted sequences of facts and rules which have previously been proved to be valid in a mathematical (or "formal") way. Let us turn to an example.

If we were given the rule

"IF Smith is a computer scientist THEN Smith is a masochist"

and assume the simple fact

"Smith is a computer scientist"

then it may seem natural to conclude that

"Smith is a masochist"

More formally, we are applying the logical pattern

IF P THEN Q, P THEREFORE Q

where the letters "P" and "Q" stand for the two sentences "Smith is a computer scientist" and "Smith is a masochist", respectively. Finding a match, we may declare that the argument has an acceptable logical structure and thus may conclude that the conclusion that "Smith is a masochist" is valid. The argument in full is:

IF Smith is a computer-scientist THEN Smith is a masochist
  Smith is a computer-scientist
THEREFORE
  Smith is a masochist

At this point it should be noted that the English sentences which replace the letters within the argument "form" are known as the "content" of the argument. Moreover, it makes no difference to the validity of the "form" whether the content makes sense in the real world, or not. For example, the following argument is still valid, although the initial assumption may perhaps be contentious.

IF Smith is a computer scientist THEN Smith is dead
Smith is a computer scientist
THEREFORE
Smith is dead

The simple argument "form" used in the above two examples is one of the most fundamental in logic and has been given the special Latin name of "modus ponendo ponens" (usually abbreviated to "modus ponens"). It is also strongly related to the particular production system approach to knowledge processing discussed in Chapter 1 (eg Figure 1.4). The connection is as follows. The rule "IF P THEN Q" corresponds to one of the production rules, while the single proposition "P" corresponds to a fact already asserted in the database of the system which, when matched to the "IF" part of the rule, results in the assertion of "Q" as a new fact. Moreover, the complete computation cycle of the simple production system corresponds to the repeated application of the "modus ponens" arguments; conclusions are generated which in turn become facts within the database. It may thus be seen that logic has a generative as well as an evaluative capability.

The capability of logic to generate (or "infer") new information from old is of particular interest given the orientation in Chapter 1 towards viewing programming as the controlled generation of inferences. Moreover, with many years of development behind it, logic also provides a well defined and well understood formalism for representing facts and the rules for manipulating them, as will be discussed below.

2.2 PREDICATE CALCULUS AND THE REPRESENTATION OF KNOWLEDGE

In Chapter 1 a number of programs were introduced which made use of simple facts such as:

reports-to (john,jim)
manages (jim,john)

It was pointed out that such facts consisted of a single relation – given to the left of the brackets – and some objects which it relates – given within the brackets. Such structures form the basic sentences of predicate calculus and replace the single letter designations (eg "P" and "Q") used earlier in the previous section.

Within predicate calculus the relation names are termed "predicates" and the objects are termed "arguments" (which must not be confused with the previous use of the term "argument" to mean a structure relating assumptions and conclusions). Moreover, all predicate calculus structures in logic are termed "propositions", and in classical predicate calculus must either have the value "true" or "false". Thus, the propositions given in section 2.1 could have been written in predicate calculus notation as

is-a (smith,computer-scientist)
is-a (smith,masochist)
is-a (smith,dead)

An "object" may either be expressed as a "constant", indicating a particular individual or class of individuals, or as a "variable", indicating that the individual or its class remains unspecified. For example, one interpretation of

is-a (X,computer-scientist)

could be that "There is some object X that is a computer scientist". When a variable becomes filled in with the name of an object (ie a "constant"), the variable is said to be "instantiated". In our notation all constant symbols begin with a small letter.

Two additional points should be noted regarding predicates. First, the order of arguments ("smith" and "computer-scientist" in the above example) must always be defined with reference to a given interpretation of the predicate within some defined domain of interest. The programmer must therefore decide upon a fixed interpretative order at the outset and maintain it throughout. Secondly, a predicate may take any number of arguments. Up to now all predicates have been binary. However, the sentence "Smith works for IBM as a computer scientist" could be represented as a three argument predicate:

works (smith,ibm,computer-scientist)

or alternatively as

works (computer-scientist,ibm,smith)

while the sentence "The computer is broken" would be represented as a single argument predicate

broken (computer)

Individual propositions (called "atomic"), each consisting of a predicate and its related arguments, may be combined to form compound propositions by the use of "logical connectives". These include "and" (&), "or" (v), "not" (~) and "implies" (→). The "implies" connective is particularly important for our purposes because it is the connective that is used to form rules, and may have the alternative reading in English of "IF . . . THEN . . .". Here are a few examples of compound propositions using the four connectives listed above:

> is-a (smith,computer-scientist) & reads (smith,science-fiction)
> ie, "Smith is a computer scientist and reads science fiction"

> reports-to (smith,jones) → manages (jones,smith)
> ie, "If Smith reports to Jones then he is managed by Jones"

> wrote (smith,program) & ~work (program) → fix (smith,program,evening) v give (program,programmer,next-day)
> ie, "If Smith wrote the program and it does not work then he will either fix it in the evening or give it to a programmer the next day"

Given the structures listed above it is possible to express many of the facts found in a conventional employee database. Avoiding variables, which introduce an additional complexity to be discussed below, we could assert

> "Smith is a computer scientist who works for IBM as a manager. Johns and Jones are programmers managed by Smith and Johns has an additional responsibility as a technical writer".

> is-a (smith,computer-scientist)
> works (smith,ibm,manager)
> programmer (johns) & technical-writer (johns)
> programmer (jones)
> manages (smith,johns) & manages (smith,jones)

We stated above that propositions can be expressed using variables as arguments and that these take on a value when instantiated by the name of an individual object or class of object. For predicate calculus to be able to process variables there is a need for an additional structure known as a "quantifier".

Quantifiers are used to indicate how many of a variable's instantiations need to be "true" for the whole proposition to be "true". There are two types – the "universal quantifier", symbolised as "∀", and the "existential quantifier", symbolised as "∃". With universal quantification – ∀(X) – all substitutions of the variable(s) in brackets within some domain of application must be "true"; with existential quantification – ∃(X) – only some of the substitutions need be "true". One can think of universal quantification as adding the word "All" before a proposition and existential quantification as adding the word "Some". Using quantification, we can express the sentence

"All computer scientists are programmers"

as

∀(X) (computer-scientist (X) → programmer (X))

The sentence

"Some computer scientists are optimists"

may be expressed as

∃(X) (computer-scientist (X) → optimist (X))

Universal and existential quantification can be mixed within the same expression. In this case, the order with which the quantified variables are introduced may affect meaning. For example, the expression

∀(X) ∃(Y) (employee (X) → manager (Y,X))

could be read as

"Every employee has a manager"

while reversing the order of the quantifiers

∃(Y) ∀(X) (employee (X) → manager (Y,X))

will give a very different reading

"There is a person who manages everyone"

Given the representational machinery of predicate calculus, it is possible to express in a standard form many very complex English sentences. Moreover, in addition to making the meaning of such sentences unambiguous, the calculus also allows them to be transformed in different ways which maintains their meaning but perhaps makes them easier for a computer to process. Such transformation is made possible by the fact that all logical connectives may be re-expressed in terms of other connectives. For example, the compound proposition

~(~computer-scientist (smith) v ~manager (smith))

may be expressed as

computer-scientist (smith) & manager (smith)

Some may argue that the first of these is not easy to understand!

Furthermore, the rule

reports-to (jones,smith) → manages (smith, jones)

may be represented as

~reports-to (jones,smith) v manages (smith,jones)

Although harder to understand, the latter transformation is important for the automation of predicate calculus (see Chapter 9).

It is conventional, when talking about manipulations which are true by definition within predicate logic, to represent propositions by single letters. Thus, the above examples would be expressed as

A & B is the same as ~(~A v ~B)

A → B is the same as ~A v B

Whilst correct, the above propositions often seem counter intuitive and you will probably need to apply them to a number of different examples before you get a feeling for their equivalence.

A final point to make is that the function of logical connectives and quantifiers in constructing compound propositions out of simple ("atomic") propositions is governed by well-defined rules called "rules of formation". These preserve the meaning of the set of propositions, although changing their structure. These correctly formed compound propositions are termed "well-formed formulas" (or "wffs" for short). For example, the connective "and" (&) can only be placed *between* propositions.

2.3 LOGICAL INFERENCE

In order to process knowledge using predicate calculus it is essential that we be able to take some given set of facts and rules and to infer new facts and rules from them. Moreover, we would want to do this in such a way that we can be confident of the validity of the new information.

Chapter 1 opened with a discussion of the difficulty of writing a program to handle "reports-to" and "manages" relations using a conventional programming language such as PASCAL. Predicate calculus, however, is ideally suited to processing such "propositional" material. It may be recalled that we were given the facts:

Fact 1:   manages (peter,john)
Fact 2:   manages (john,ann)
Fact 3:   manages (ann,fred)

and two rules (now stated to include quantification)

Rule 1: $\forall(X,Y)$ (manages $(X,Y) \rightarrow$ reports-to (Y,X))
Rule 2: $\forall(X,Y,Z)$ (manages (X,Y) & reports-to $(Z,Y) \rightarrow$ reports-to (Z,X))

These rules may be read as

"For all X and Y, if X manages Y then Y reports-to X"

"For all X, Y and Z, if X manages Y, and Z reports-to Y, then Z reports-to X"

respectively.

Taking a simpler example than that described in Chapter 1, we will use the above rules to see if we can generate the inference that "Fred reports-to John". It will readily be seen, however, that the inference cannot be made directly by a simple application of either of the rules. It is thus necessary to approach the problem indirectly by first using Rule 1 and Fact 3 to generate the intermediate inference

reports-to (fred,ann)

and then using this inferred fact along with Rule 2 and Fact 2 conclude the desired fact

reports-to (fred,john)

Indeed, our inferences do not have to stop here. A further application of Rule 2 along with this conclusion and Fact 1 will allow the additional inference

reports-to (fred,peter)

From this description it may appear that the only rules we have used to make the inference are Rules 1 and 2. However, this is not the case. The reader has in fact implicitly made use of two higher-level rules which in logic are termed "rules of inference". In the above instance these rules are so intuitively obvious that the reader may be forgiven for not noticing that they are there at all. The first of these is the "modus ponens" rule which we have mentioned before

$$A \rightarrow B, \ A \ |- B \ (\text{"} |- \text{" is called "turnstile" and can be read as}$$
$$\text{"THEREFORE")}$$

The other rule is called "universal specialisation" and is written as

$$\forall(X) \ W \ (X), \ A \ |- W \ (A)$$

The rule is used to define the meaning of the universal quantifier and, although it may look complex, simply captures the intuition that if some class of object has a property, any individual within that class will also have that property.

Rules of inference are very general statements of the relationships between assumptions and conclusions that are universally valid for predicate calculus. Indeed, we have introduced the idea of "rule of inference" earlier in this chapter (section 2.1) when we talked of logical "forms" and, in particular, the form of a "modus ponens" argument. Applied to correctly formed sentences (or "wffs") of predicate calculus in any domain, they will yield other correctly formed predicate calculus sentences. As such, they contrast with rules such as Rule 1 and Rule 2 in the program which are known as "domain rules", their validity being restricted to the current domain of "reporting-to" and "managing". The rules of inference can be thought of as part of a general control structure within which we manipulate the domain rules.

In the present example, the "modus ponens" rule of inference is simply used to apply the facts (including inferred facts) as the conditions of the domain rules in order to generate new facts, these being the conclusion of the rules. For example, given the rule that "If an object is an ungulate then it will eat grass" and the fact that "A horse is an ungulate", the "modus ponens" rule enables us to conclude that "Horses eat grass". As stated above, the rule of "universal specialisation" governs the instantiation of variables and captures the notion that if some class of objects has a property, then a member of the class will also have that property.

Within predicate calculus there are many different rules of inference. Being universally true of the calculus, they may be used either to validate complete arguments or to generate conclusions. Moreover, individual rules of inference may either be used on their own, or may be applied in conjunction with others. A list of a few basic rules is given in Figure 2.1.

1) Modus ponendo ponens (MPP): $A \longrightarrow B$, $A \mid - B$

2) Modus tollendo tollens (MTT): $A \longrightarrow B$, $\sim B \mid - \sim A$ (eg, IF My program is correct THEN it will run, My program will NOT run THEREFORE it is not correct)

3) Double negation (DN): $A \mid - \sim(\sim A)$ (eg, My program has run THEREFORE My program has NOT NOT run)

4) &introduction (&INT): $A, B \mid - (A \& B)$ (eg, My program has run, It is correct THEREFORE MY program has run AND is correct)

5) Reductio ad absurdum (RAA): $A \longrightarrow B$, $A \longrightarrow \sim B \mid - \sim A$ (eg, IF My program is correct THEN It will run, IF My program is correct THEN It will NOT run THEREFORE My program is not correct)

6) Universal specialisation (US): $\forall(X) W(X)$, $A \mid - W(A)$ (eg All things which are computers are unreliable, a "TIPTOP" is a computer THEREFORE a "TIP-TOP" is unreliable)

Figure 2.1   Some Basic Inference Rules

Let us now look at an example in which we are given a simple rule

"IF computer science is a growing subject THEN there is *no* shortage of applicants"

growing (computer-science) $\rightarrow \sim$ shortage (computer-science, applicants)

and a simple fact that there is a "shortage of applicants",

shortage (computer-science, applicants)

Given this information, we wish to discover whether it can be concluded that "Computer science is *not* a growing subject", ie

$\sim$growing (computer-science)

To do this, we start from the assumed fact and rule, and apply a rule of inference to see if we can generate the desired conclusion. If this is not possible, some rule of inference is applied to produce an intermediate result, which may then be used along with the original information as the basis for the application of further rules of inference. In the example, it is not possible to derive the conclusion by a single application of the "rules of inference" given in Figure 2.1. However, it can be done in two stages. The first move is to generate an intermediate inference by applying the "rule of double negation" (DN) to the simple fact

shortage (computer-science,applicants)

to yield the equivalent fact

~(~shortage (computer-science,applicants))

Having generated this new fact we can use it along with the domain rule

growing (computer-science) → ~shortage (computer-science, applicants)

and the "modus tollens" (MTT) rule to yield the desired conclusion

~growing (computer-science)

The reader may have had difficulty in following this last inference, given the statement of the "modus tollens" rule in Figure 2.1. We will therefore go through it again using letters for the main propositions for the sake of clarity.

Assuming that

A = growing (computer-science)
B = shortage (computer-science,applicants)

our rule and fact can be expressed as

A → ~B
B

the conclusion we wish to prove as being true is

~A

The first move is to generate an intermediate result by applying the rule of "double negation" to B, producing

~(~B)   (ie, ~(~B) ≡ B)

The second move is to use the "modus tollens" rule (Figure 2.1) which is (using C and D as general propositions)

$$C \to D, \sim D \mid - \sim C$$

or equivalently

$$C \to \sim D, \sim(\sim D) \mid - \sim C$$

Therefore, if we are given $C \to \sim D$ and $\sim(\sim D)$, we can conclude that $\sim C$ is true. But this is the pattern we observe with our original propositions. Thus $A \to \sim B$ and $\sim(\sim B)$ will enable us to conclude $\sim A$.

This proof is summarised in Figure 2.2.

$A \longrightarrow \sim B, B \mid - \sim A$

		JUSTIFICATION	RULE
(1)	$A \longrightarrow \sim B$	Given	
(2)	B	Given	
(3)	$\sim(\sim B)$	(2)	DN
(4)	$\sim A$	(1,3)	MTT

Figure 2.2   Formal Structure of a Proof

An important characteristic of predicate calculus which was mentioned in the previous section is that there are many different ways of asserting the same thing. It was, for example, pointed out that the conjunctive proposition

A & B

is equivalent to the negated disjunctive proposition

$\sim(\sim A \vee \sim B)$

Moreover we used this feature in the above proof with reference to the description of the "modus tollens" rule of inference.

The same characteristic applies to complete proofs, it often being possible to evaluate an argument in a number of different ways. The proof conducted in Figure 2.2, using the inference rules of "double negation" and "modus tollens", could have been conducted using the rules of "modus ponens", "&introduction" and "reductio ad absurdum" – see Figure 2.3.

A ⟶ ~B, B |– ~A

		JUSTIFICATION	RULE
(1)	A ⟶ ~B	Given	
(2)	B	Given	
(3)	A	Assumed	
(4)	~B	(1,3)	MPP
(5)	B &~B	(2,4)	&INT
(6)	~A	(3,5)	RAA

Figure 2.3   An Alternative Proof of A ⟶ ~B, B |– ~A

The new proof is not really so elegant as the previous one but is in fact actually formally equivalent.

2.4   PROBLEMS WITH PREDICATE CALCULUS FOR KNOWLEDGE PROCESSING

The proofs given in figures in the previous section demonstrated that it is possible within predicate calculus to generate a set of inferences in order to prove the validity of a conclusion by applying the "rules of inference" to the domain facts and rules asserted about the problem. However, given our concern with knowledge processing, we are interested in the automation of this process, and it turns out that there are a number of fundamental difficulties in doing this. For example there is a difficulty over the nature of the reasoning process in predicate calculus when compared with common-sense reasoning. Furthermore, whilst a proof looks straightforward in retrospect (when we can appreciate it "bottom-up" from assumptions to conclusions) it is not clear from the completed proof how we decided which rules of inference to apply, or when to apply them.

The first difficulty concerns the way that classical predicate calculus makes assumptions about the relationship between conditions and conclusions which do not apply to common sense reasoning. With predicate calculus it is never necessary to withdraw any conclusions when additional facts become known. For example, if we had proved that

$A \rightarrow C$

then C will continue to be true given *any* additional fact B

ie $A \& B \rightarrow C$

In technical language, predicate calculus is "monotonic", meaning that conclusions are additive and never need to be revised.

This monotonic feature is clearly not acceptable in the real world. Although we would be happy with the rule

"IF engine is overheating THEN immediately switch off engine"

we may question the wisdom of the rule

"IF engine is overheating AND driving in fast lane of motorway THEN immediately switch off engine"

In real life we often have to modify or withdraw conclusions as new facts become available. Formal systems which enable this to be done are said to be "non-monotonic".

Regarding automation, one unintelligent approach, which would never be adopted in practice, would be simply to apply inference rules blindly in the hope that a "proof" would eventually emerge. However, with such a simplistic procedure it would be unrealistic to expect the program to run in real time. For a start, many proofs depend upon making additional assumptions at some point to enable a rule to be applied at some later stage. The computer would thus need to have expectations concerning its future actions. A second problem is that the blind application of some perfectly valid inference rules will lead to a "combinatorial explosion". For example, the repeated application of the "& inclusion" rule to the three propositions P,Q and R could generate an infinite number of compound propositions, including such odd (and uninteresting) ones as:

(P&Q) & (P&Q) & (P&Q)
P&Q&Q&Q&Q&R

In order to automate predicate calculus proofs, it will be clear that it is necessary to define some procedure for deciding what rules to apply which prevents combinatorial explosion and which allows for non-monotonic reasoning. Much work in the 1960s within both logic and

Artificial Intelligence was directed at finding such "effective procedures", as they are termed. These approaches took one of two directions.

The first approach to the problem of control, which was largely adopted within the discipline of Artificial Intelligence, abandoned the principle of generality and sought processing techniques which were effective for some specific problem within a defined problem domain. With these techniques, processing power is largely derived from the large amount of domain specific knowledge coded into a system and follows the observation that human expert problem-solvers rarely use very general procedures but gain effectiveness from "knowing" more about the problem. In order to make it easier to program such "knowledge-based" systems, researchers have developed formalisms which are weaker in expressive power than predicate calculus, but which are more amenable to computation. These will be discussed next in Chapter 3. Many of these approaches were developed using the list processing language, LISP.

The second approach continued within the tradition of logic in that it attempted to maintain the generality of predicate calculus by identifying proof procedures which are universal but which avoid the problem of rule selection and combinatorial explosion. This approach has mainly been of interest within logic itself, the investigation of methods for automation of proof (termed "theorem proving") being a study in its own right. Until recently, many of the methods discovered were too inefficient to be used for practical purposes. However, within recent years the programming language PROLOG has been developed as the combination of one theorem proving method – "resolution theorem proving" – and a particularly efficient control strategy which will be discussed in detail in Chapter 9. Thus, there is now available an automated version of predicate calculus which may be used as a general-purpose language for knowledge programming.

3 Computational Approaches to Representation and Control

3.1 THE SHIFT TO KNOWLEDGE-BASED SYSTEMS

The approach to information processing from which expert systems technology developed differed from that pursued by logicians in that it sought techniques for the control of inference which were specific to a particular knowledge domain. With reference to our discussion of predicate calculus, this may be understood in terms of removing the distinction between domain rules and inference rules. The two classes of procedural knowledge kept separate within predicate calculus in order to maintain generality are replaced by rules defined with varying degrees of generality with reference to some domain. Such rules are then applied within a control framework appropriate to the structure of that domain. It necessarily follows that systems developed in this tradition will be domain specific.

The need for a "knowledge-based" approach to information processing had already been recognised within Artificial Intelligence, principally with reference to symbolic problem-solving. Many of the fundamental concepts and techniques evolved from work on automated game playing (ranging from simple games such as noughts-and-crosses to complex games such as chess) and natural language understanding. In both of these broad domains, it was found that in order to approach human performance, it was necessary to code considerable domain knowledge into systems. Moreover, this strategy has been validated by actual studies of human processing in these areas; chess masters, for example, owe their superior performance to their memory of very many patterns of chess positions and the implications of those positions, rather than their superior ability to apply a few powerful deductive procedures.

The shift of emphasis from the problems of building powerful general-purpose "inference engines" to those of automating human knowledge led inevitably to a new set of interests. The first of these concerned the development of formalisms for representing factual and procedural knowledge in such a way as to make explicit those aspects which were critical to a particular problem. It was found, for example, in natural language understanding research that in order for a program to resolve many of the ambiguities that exist in written text, it was necessary for the system to represent an outline of the events or situations under consideration. This may be illustrated with the following passage concerning events in a restaurant:

> "Having enjoyed his portion of duck, John called to the waiter and asked for the bill. It was brought on a plate and, to John's dismay, was considerably larger than expected. He should have taken his friends' warning and been careful of what he ordered."

The text contains one major ambiguity concerning the word "bill". If interpreted in its immediate context it has two possible meanings; either the beak of the duck or the account for the cost of the meal. Furthermore, the rest of the passage could be read to suggest either of these interpretations.

However, if we were to interpret the passage in the broader context of the sequence of events that typically take place in restaurants, it is likely that there would be no ambiguity. The scenario usually includes paying for the meal after one has been presented with the "bill" as a statement of account for the food and drink consumed. The "common-sense" interpretation would thus be of the "bill" being a "statement of account", and a computer system interpreting the passage would therefore need to have knowledge of the typical events taking place in a restaurant in order to reach this common-sense interpretation.

There may, of course, be situations in which the alternative interpretation might just possibly be correct, eg where the meal was being eaten in an exotic Chinese restaurant where "duck bill" might be a candidate ingredient. A really smart system with knowledge of such exceptions to the norm would pick this up – and an even smarter system might laugh! In this case some alternative method of disambiguation would have to be employed other than the simple operation of inspecting a record of typical events. For example, the system could use general knowledge concerning "duck bills" in order to prove that they were "edible" under certain circumstances, using very general rules about their composition and the effect of cooking on them. Having deduced that duck bills are "edible" when boiled to make a soup, the system might then choose this alternative explanation.

Although we will not consider in detail issues of knowledge representation until later in this chapter, a couple of points may be usefully mentioned at this stage. First, it is important to note that in the example the problem of disambiguation is solved using domain knowledge concerning activities typically taking place in restaurants, the qualities of duck bills, general information about cooking, etc. Secondly, even though the duck bill interpretation is possible under certain circumstances it is unlikely in the general case. In order to maximise the speed of processing, the most likely interpretation will be explicitly represented leaving the more unlikely interpretations to be inferred.

The representation of knowledge is only one of the concerns underlying knowledge programming. A second, which has been hinted at in the above paragraph, is that of controlling the application of knowledge; while the design of a control structure will be partially dependent upon choices made in the representation of knowledge, it must also reflect other factors, the principal one being possible "decompositions" of the problem.

The ease with which a problem may be solved is in part related to the extent to which it can be decomposed into a number of more simply solved sub-problems. Moreover, the extent of decomposition and the nature of the relationship that exists between sub-problems will influence the general control structure which may be applied to the problem. This may be illustrated by the problem expressed by a walker trying to get to the top of a mountain.

Let us assume that our walker suddenly finds himself shrouded in mist and has only a compass to guide him. One simple strategy he may follow is to take a step along each of the four cardinal points N, S, E and W and then to move finally in the direction which feels as if it is leading upwards – "best-step" rule. This control strategy is illustrated in Figure 3.1.

However, the success of this strategy is very dependent upon the environment in which it is executed. If there are a number of foothills, our walker following this strategy may find himself at the top of a local peak rather than at the top of the main mountain. Having got into this situation, the walker would need some additional control machinery to enable

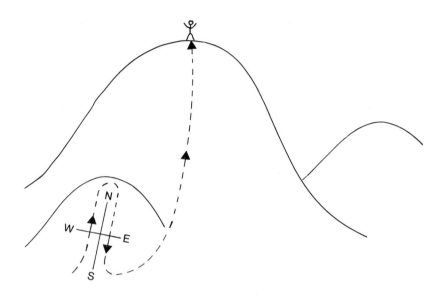

Figure 3.1   A "Best-Step" Mountain Climbing Strategy (With Backtracking)

him to proceed. Two of a number of possibilities are as follows. A simple strategy is to "backtrack" to the point where he started to climb the local hill, take a step in some alternative direction, and then continue to apply the "best-step" rule.

A further alternative may become possible if the mist cleared for a second when our walker was on the local peak and he glimpsed his goal ahead of him. He would then be able to apply a strategy of striking off towards the peak, even if this meant that he would have to lose height temporarily. In other words, the increased information that the glimpse of the mountain gave him would give him confidence to pursue the different goal of losing height so that he would be in a better position to climb again at some later period.

The main point to remember from the above example is that the "control structure" used for relating domain knowledge must take account of the structure of that knowledge. In the present instance, a "mountain climbing" control structure which would work in an environment without foothills could not be guaranteed to work in an environment with foothills. Here a more complex technique involving "back-tracking" or "look-ahead" would be required.

3.2 LISP – A LANGUAGE FOR PROGRAMMING KNOWLEDGE-BASED SYSTEMS

In order to implement the objectives of the previous section, designers of knowledge based systems needed a language that was more flexible than the conventional languages, and a new functional programming language – LISP – was developed to satisfy this need.

The LISP programming language is based upon work conducted by John McCarthy during the 1960s on non-numeric computation. Since then it has undergone considerable development and now it is the *lingua franca* of Artificial Intelligence.

LISP stands for LISt Programming language. This reflects the fact that the fundamental structure of LISP is the "list", a list being made up of a combination of abstract symbols, called "atoms".

An "atom" is the most fundamental program object and therefore itself has no component parts, as the name implies. However, an "atom" does have a name, such as "MANAGES", "JOHN", "SMITH" and "NIL", and may itself have attributes or properties attached to it. The most important of these is termed its "value". This is rather like a variable having a value in a conventional programming language.

A list in LISP is made up of some combination of atoms (possibly zero) enclosed in parentheses. For example, the expression

(MANAGES JOHN PETER)

is a correctly formed LISP expression, consisting of a list of three atoms – MANAGES, JOHN and PETER. Likewise the expression

(AND (COMPUTER-SCIENTIST JOHN) (READS JOHN SCIENCE-FICTION))

is a list, having embedded within it two additional lists. Each unit of the list is termed an "element" and in this example the first element is an atom, the second is a list of two atoms and the third is a list of three atoms. One final point about lists is that they are terminated by the special atom "NIL". This stands for the "null" or "empty" list. This list terminator is not shown in normal list syntax.

The processing of LISP expressions – termed "S-expressions" – may be achieved using only five primitive functions. While LISP systems in fact provide many more functions than these, many of them may be built from these five. They are

CAR — gives the value of the first element of a list, eg the CAR of (MANAGES JOHN PETER) is the atom "MANAGES"

CDR — gives the value of a list without the first element, eg the CDR of (MANAGES JOHN PETER) is the list (JOHN PETER)

CONS — joins two expressions to form list structures, eg the CONS of the atom "MANAGES" and the list (JOHN) is the list (MANAGES JOHN); the CONS of the two atoms "MANAGES" and "JOHN" is a special type of list, (MANAGES . JOHN); the CONS of the atom "JOHN" and the empty list ( ) is the list (JOHN)

ATOM — gives the value "true" if applied to an atom, otherwise gives the value "false", eg ATOM applied to "MANAGES" would have the value "true" – T, while ATOM applied to the list (JOHN PETER) would have the value "false" – NIL

EQUAL — gives the value "true" if two expressions are equal, otherwise gives the value "false", eg if the two atoms "JOHN" and "PETER" are compared using EQUAL, the result will be "false", but the comparison of "JOHN" with "JOHN" yields "true".

LISP programs consist of sets of functions. The control structure of a program is thus largely "applicative", in that it is guided by the application of functions to arguments, which may in themselves be functions. This is very different from the sequential control of conventional programming languages discussed in Chapter 1.

In order to define useful functions, two additional higher-level structures are required. These are "DEFUN", which is used to create the actual function definition, and "COND" which is the LISP version of the conditional. Both of these primitive functions are employed in the following example of the function "BOSS", which is used to check whether a "MANAGES" relationship exists between two individuals in an employee database. Facts in this database are of the form (RELATION PERSON1 PERSON2).

```
(DEFUN BOSS (FACT)
   (COND
      ((EQUAL (CAR FACT) 'MANAGES) T)
      ( T NIL)          ) )
```

The term "DEFUN" indicates that the code which follows will be a function definition, the atom in parentheses following "DEFUN" being the parameter to be passed to the function. In the present instance let us assume that it is applied to the fact

(MANAGES JOHN PETER)

Within the function "BOSS" there is nested a single conditional indicated by the function name "COND". Each line of code following "COND" may be read as a separate "IF . . . THEN . . ." statement. "COND" evaluates by moving down the list of statements, evaluating the "IF" part. The first that evaluates to something other than false – NIL – causes the evaluation of the corresponding THEN part. In the present instance, the first IF part evaluates to "true", the CAR of the list (MANAGES JOHN PETER) being equal to "MANAGES". The resulting atom is presented as an argument to the function "EQUAL", along with a second argument, the quoted atom "MANAGES". (The quote mark ', which we see here for the first time, tells the interpreter that the object quoted is a data item, not a parameter whose current value should be sought and used.) Thus the two arguments are tested for equality. This is found to be "true", causing the THEN part of the statement to be evaluated; being the special atom "T", the whole procedure will then return the value "true".

If the FACT submitted to the function had been

(REPORTS-TO JOHN PETER)

the first "IF" statement would have failed, ie evaluated to NIL. In this case, the COND would have proceeded to evaluate the next statement. Since in this case we have forced the final IF condition to always be TRUE, the THEN part delivers "false", ie NIL. The statement is thus rejected.

Most of the programs to be discussed in this book are implemented in LISP and the methods they use to represent facts and domain specific procedural knowledge thus employ LISP constructs. The most prominent of these is the "property list". Simply stated, each "atom" may have "properties" associated with it. These may be defined by the programmer and provide a convenient method of representing associations between objects. A "property" is defined as a "property/value" pair which is linked to an "atom". For example, the atom "SMITH" may be given the property "READS" and value "SCIENCE-FICTION". The generality of the property list structure has proved valuable for constructing specialised forms of knowledge representation which will be discussed in the following sections.

3.3 THE REPRESENTATION OF DOMAIN KNOWLEDGE

3.3.1 Semantic Networks

Semantic network notation is based on the ancient and very simple idea that "memory" is composed of associations between concepts. The notion of an "associative memory" has been traced as far back as Aristotle, and it made its entrance into computer science through work on the use of simple associations for representing word meaning in databases. Since then the formalism has been widely explored for the representation of many classes of information in many different subject areas. Subject areas explored include spatial relations in simple physical worlds, manipulative operations, causal and functional relations within mechanical devices and relations between medical symptoms.

The basic functional unit of a semantic network is a structure consisting of two points, of "nodes", linked by an "arc". Each node represents some concept and the arc represents a relation between pairs of concepts. Such pairs of related concepts may be thought of as representing a simple fact. Nodes are labelled with the name of the relevant relation. Figure 3.2, for example, represents the fact that:

"Smith works in the production department"

Figure 3.2   A Functional Unit of a Semantic Network

Note that the arc is directed, thus preserving the "subject/object" relation between the concepts within the fact.

Moreover, any node may be linked to any number of other nodes, so giving rise to a formation of a network of facts.

With reference to our earlier discussion of logic, the basic semantic network structure may be seen as equivalent to a predicate with two arguments (a binary predicate), the two arguments being represented by the two nodes, and the predicate by the directed arc linking them.

The judicious choice of relational labels permits the expression of very complex groups of facts. A label of particular practical importance in the development of semantic network representation is the "is-a" link, which is used to indicate membership of some class of objects. The network unit in Figure 3.3, for example, asserts that:

"Smith is a member of the class of managers"

or said more normally:

"Smith is a manager"

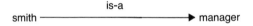

Figure 3.3   The "is-a" Relation

Other links of particular use for describing object concepts (those normally given as nouns and noun phrases) are "has", indicating that one concept is a part of the other; and "is", indicating that one concept is an attribute of the other. Using such relations, it is possible to represent complex sets of facts. Figure 3.4 illustrates one possible representation of facts about an employee "smith". These include:

"Smith is a manager"
"Smith works in the Production Department located in Building-1"
"Smith is 40 years old"
"Smith has blue eyes"

From the diagrams it may be seen that quite complex sets of information may be built up from network units.

In LISP the basic semantic network unit may be programmed as an

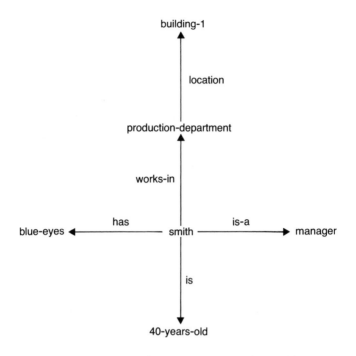

Figure 3.4   Facts about a Man named "smith"

atom/property list combination. The unit given in Figure 3.2 would be composed of "smith" as the atom, "works-in" as a property and "production-department" as the value of that property. The value "production-department" is, of course, an atom in its own right, and this may have a property list associated with it as well. Hence we may represent the location of the "production-department" as the property "location" and value "building-1" on the property list of the atom "production-department".

It was not possible in the basic semantic network notations to represent situations where a number of separate objects were instances of the same general concept. For example, it may be necessary to record that a company employs two different people called "smith", one of whom works for the manager "smith" and is "staff" rather than management. A network using an extended notation is given in Figure 3.5.

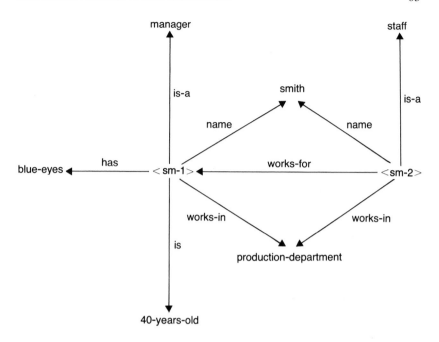

Figure 3.5   Facts about "sm-1" and "sm-2"

The solution is to use two special nodes, labelled "<sm-1>" and "<sm-2>", to identify the two different individuals who share the name "smith". The distinction between specific objects and general concepts is fundamental in the use of semantic networks. The two different kinds of object have therefore been given different names. A specific object is termed a "token" (we have used the notation of Norman and Rumelhart by employing angle brackets – < > – to identify token nodes); a general concept is termed a "type" and has no special identifier.

Much of the early popularity of semantic networks arose from the processing power provided by the "is-a" link to build up hierarchies of concepts. A fairly typical example is the "employee" node in Figure 3.6, which is an augmented version of Figure 3.5. Here we have a shallow hierarchy of concepts, with "employee" at the root and the two individuals "<sm-1>" and "<sm-2>" as terminals. Now, given such a hierarchy, it is possible to distribute through the network general facts relating to individuals which are directly attributable to their being members of classes of employee, instead of attributing them directly to individuals. Examples of such facts might be that "employees" are entitled to "parking permits" and that "managers" have a "key" to the "office door". The relevant extensions are given in Figure 3.6. These facts will still be accessible from the token nodes representing individuals by "inheritance" via the "is-a" links.

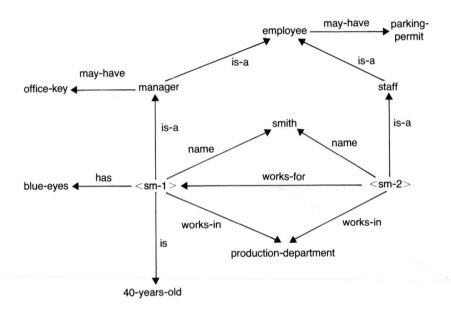

Figure 3.6   Facts about the Employees named "smith"

Inheritance hierarchies provide an effective way of simplifying our representation, and of reducing the information we are required to store at any particular node. This considerably speeds processing (information stored at a node may be limited to that which is most frequently required, leaving other information to be accessed via inheritance) and to permit information retrieval given general queries (some information about "smith" as a manager may be retrieved simply from knowledge of his position in the company without needing to know his name).

The examples of semantic network representation given so far have been limited to binary relations between nouns (or noun phrases). However, this is a severe limitation. Many of the facts that we may want to use in a knowledge-based program will be concerned with "events", these often being bounded by limits of time or space. For instance, it might be necessary to assert that:

"Smith-2 worked for Smith-1 from April, 1972 to May, 1983"

It is not possible to represent this in the notation given so far as it is equivalent to a 4-argument "work-for" predicate. The solution is very simple, and extremely powerful. What is required is to develop representations around verbs in addition to nouns. Still maintaining our distinction between types and tokens, a verbal token node comes to represent a specific event, while a type verb node represents a "prototype" event. The resulting network is given in Figure 3.7.

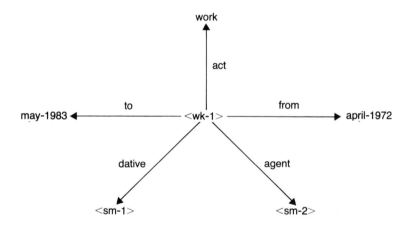

Figure 3.7   Event Representation Organised around a Verb

The specific event of working for someone has been labelled "wk-1", and takes its identity as an event from the prototype node "work" via the arc "act". We have generalised the convention of surrounding token nodes with angle brackets to include event nodes. Note that the "act" arc is the event equivalent of the "is-a" arc. Having identified the specific event – "wk-1", it is now possible to attach binary relations to it to represent aspects of working, such as start date – via the "from" link, and end date – via the "to" link.

Consistent and comprehensive sets of verbal relations have been developed for individual systems. These are usually termed "case relations" after the theory of "Case Grammar" developed by Fillmore. Briefly, the theory attempts to account for the surface structure of sentences in terms of a small, closed set of relationships – "cases" – between nouns (or noun phrases) and verbs held to exist within the deep structure of sentences. A sample set of relations may typically include that of:

a) AGENT – the initiator of the action identified by the verb;

b) OBJECT – the noun affected by the action or state identified by the verb;

c) LOCATION – the location of the action or state identified by the verb;

d) DATIVE – the person affected by the state or action identified by the verb.

As mentioned above, the event pointed to by the "act" link has the character of a "prototype". As such, it could be represented as in Figure 3.8.

Here the case labels on the arcs point to variables, which for an actual

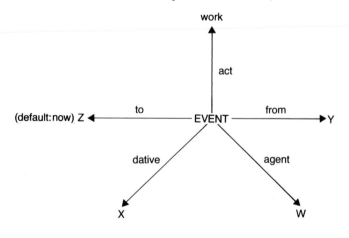

Figure 3.8 A Prototype "work" Event

event would take on the value of the actual nouns (or noun phrases) participating in that event. In the present instance these are "sm-1", "sm-2", "april-1972" and "may-1983". Prototype structures come very close to the "frame" representations to be described in the next section, and may be used to advantage in processing. Two important applications include using the case labels to help identify the sentence objects to be bound to variables (this would give a system some measure of "expectation"), and giving variables "default values", which will be the values that the variables will take in the absence of an explicitly alternative value being available to the system (this would allow a system to proceed in the absence of explicit input). In Figure 3.8, the "to" relation has been given the default that the person will still be employed – (default:now) – to be used in the absence of specific information that the employee has left.

3.3.2 Frames

The idea of organising the properties of some object or event to form a prototype is formalised in the notion of a "frame". To illustrate this we will describe information on the employees of a company as we did in the previous section. The strength of frame systems lies in the fact that those elements that are conventionally present in the description of an object or event are grouped together and may thus be accessed and processed as a unit. The first example will be that of a general concept – "manager" (see Figure 3.9).

name :   MANAGER

       specialisation-of : EMPLOYEE

       name : _____

       age : _____

       address : _____

       department : _____

       salary : _____

       start-date : _____

       to : _____

Figure 3.9   A Skeleton Frame for the Concept "MANAGER"

Figure 3.9 illustrates a number of points about frame systems. First, the frame has a name which identifies the concept it describes. Secondly, the description itself is made up of a set of descriptions, given to the left of the figure, which are termed "slots" and identify the basic structural elements of the concept. Next to these slots there are spaces which may be filled by some object which represents the current value of the slot. All the slots in Figure 3.9 are displayed empty except for the first, which has the value "EMPLOYEE". The slot name "specialisation-of" indicates that the current frame represents a concept which bears a subset relationship to the concept names in the slot value. The "specialisation-of" slot is therefore used to set up an inheritance hierarchy in a similar manner to the "is-a" link in semantic networks. EMPLOYEE will therefore exist as a higher-level frame.

In Figure 3.10 we see the same frame but with all the slots filled. However, you will have noticed that some are filled with objects other than simple names. There are three different types of filler in the example.

A slot filler can either be a constant or the name of another frame. The simplest are those given in capital letters (eg ADDRESS, SALARY) which refer to other frames within a system of frames. In addition, there

name :   MANAGER

specialisation-of : EMPLOYEE

name : unit (family-name,first-name,initial)

age : unit (years)

address : ADDRESS

department : range (production,administration)

salary : SALARY

start-date : unit (month,year)

to : unit ((month,year) (default:now))

Figure 3.10   A Frame for the General Concept "MANAGER"

are the labels "unit" and "range". During the processing of frame systems, it is often useful to be able to set restrictions on the type(s) of object that may fill a slot. The labels "unit" and "range" provide standard restrictions: "unit" specifies that certain objects are required to be given; "range" specifies the set of objects from which one must be selected. This information may be used, for example, to drive a question asking program which inputs information to an "employee" database. Finally, default values are attached to the unit and range fillers and are given in parentheses. The frame labels "unit", "range" and "default" are called the "facets" of the slot.

A further example of a frame is given in Figure 3.11 for the "SALARY" filler of the "MANAGER" frame. It has four slots, one of which (tax-to-date) requires a double filler.

name :   SALARY

    rate-of-pay : unit (£.pa)

    tax-code : unit ((tax-code) (default:emergency))

    tax-to-date : unit (month,year)
              compute ((TAX-PAID) (tax))

Figure 3.11   A Frame for the General Concept "SALARY"

This is given to illustrate the concept of "procedural attachment", which enables conventional programs to be embedded in frames. Embedded procedures are called by a "compute" facet filler. Under the "tax-to-date" slot in the "SALARY" frame, we find the filler "compute (TAX-PAID) (tax)". This indicates that the SALARY filler is to access the TAX-PAID frame, which contains a procedure. This procedure will then be run using information from the frame system as data to compute the value of "tax-to-date", which may then be inserted in the "tax" field of the slot. It might also be noted that this frame includes one default value, indicating that in the absence of a specified tax code, the code should be given as "emergency".

As stated above, frames are usually organised into networks representing the structure of the general concepts within the subject area of interest. Given such a record of general concepts, this leaves the problem of how to represent information pertaining to individuals. The standard technique is to take a copy of the relevant parts of the system, and to instantiate it by giving values to slots relevant to the individual. Figure 3.12 is an example of the frame given in Figure 3.10 instantiated to describe the employee "smith", named "sm-1".

name :   sm-1

        specialisation-of : EMPLOYEE

        name : smith, john, h

        age : 40

        address : adr-1

        department : production

        salary : sal-1

        start-date : april-1972

        to : now

Figure 3.12   An Instantiated "MANAGER" Frame

Note that when a frame is instantiated with information relevant to an individual, it is given a unique name – in this case "sm-1" – which identifies the individual in question. This name may be used in conjunction with the names of other frame classes given as slot fillers to access additional related information. In the case of our example, the name "sm-1" would be used with the general frame names "sal-1" and "adr-1" to identify salary and address information of "smith, john, h".

Frames are relatively easily implemented using the LISP property list structure discussed previously with reference to semantic networks. Each of the states and fillers of a frame is implemented as a property list (the slot name being represented as the "property" and the filler as the "value"), each one being attached to an atom representing the frame name.

The frame idea has also been applied to many different types of problem and, according to the problem, has been subject to many variations. Chapter 8 will describe one application in the design of an expert system for the design of experiments in genetics (MOLGEN). Other applications include systems for the understanding of written text, the most notable in this area being that of Schank and his group at Yale using frame-like structures termed "scripts" which represent stereotyped sequences of events. A typical script, for example, would describe the event of going to a restaurant, this including such moves as entering the restaurant, finding a table, ordering food, eating it, asking for the bill, paying and leaving. There are also a number of languages especially designed to assist in the construction of frame-based knowledge manipulation. These include a language named KRL developed for work in natural language understanding, and the UNITS package used for MOLGEN.

3.3.3 Production Rules

The most popular format for representing knowledge in a way that maintains its procedural character is the "production rule" which is simply a single statement program of the form:

"IF condition THEN action"

The notion of writing procedures in the form of sequences of rules was first proposed by the mathematician Post. However, in order to enable the idea to be applied to real knowledge-processing problems there have been a wide range of developments, particularly with reference to the organisation of rules and in the design of control structures which manipulate them. The action part of a rule may be required to ask a question of the user, implement some standard programming procedure, or even interact with some physical device to switch the system on and off, in addition to alteration of the database.

As discussed in Chapter 1, production systems have three components: a knowledge base consisting of a set of production rules, a database which represents the current state of some problem and a control structure (in programming terms, this is known as an interpreter) which decides which production rule to apply.

The simple idea behind a set of production rules is that they define a set of allowed transformations which move a problem from its initial state-

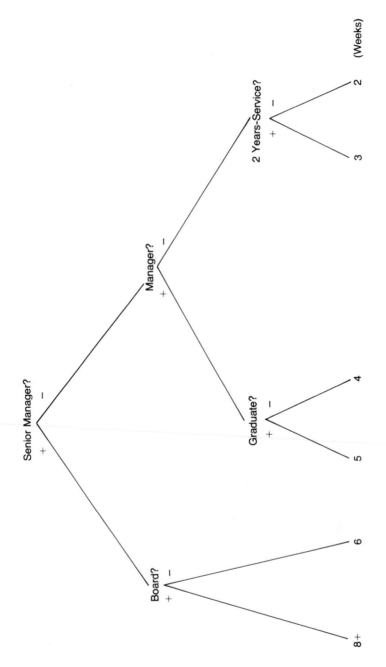

Figure 3.13   A "Holiday" Decision Tree

ment to its solution. The current state of a solution is represented by the set of facts asserted in a database. The solution progresses by the matching of one side of a rule to the database (either left- or right-hand side). Clearly in any realistic system, it is likely that a number of rules may be applicable at any one time. Thus, some control structure will be required to decide which rule to fire.

To illustrate the operation of a production system, we describe a system which implements a decision tree for deciding upon the period of holiday allowed to staff. The program is after Bundy, and is able to identify the holiday period allowed to a given member of staff, given five staff attributes.

The decision tree (Figure 3.13) is represented as a set of rules. These prompt questions in order to identify the class of employee and to aid identification. There are two additional rules, one (A) to declare a solution to the user and the other (B) to insert employee attributes into the database.

Rule A: IF "holiday period" has been identified
THEN print value of holiday period

Rule B: IF attribute "attri" has been asked & answer 'YES'
THEN delete "YES" & add attribute "attri" to database

Class 1   IF attribute "SENIOR-MANAGER" & attribute "BOARD"
Rule: THEN add that period is "8 weeks" to database.

Ques 1   IF attribute "SENIOR-MANAGER" & not asked if on "BOARD"
Rule: THEN ask "BOARD"? & add that asked "BOARD" to database & attend to answer.

Class 2   IF attribute "SENIOR-MANAGER"
Rule: THEN add that period is "6-WEEKS" to database.

Ques 2   IF not asked whether is "SENIOR-MANAGER"
Rule: THEN ask "SENIOR-MANAGER"? & add that asked "SENIOR-MANAGER" to database & attend to answer.

Class 3   IF attribute "MANAGER" & attribute "GRADUATE"
Rule: THEN add that period is "5-WEEKS" to database.

Ques 3   IF attribute "MANAGER" & not asked whether "GRADUATE"

Rule:	THEN ask "GRADUATE"? & add that asked "GRADU-ATE" to database & attend to answer.
Class 4 Rule:	IF attribute "MANAGER" THEN add that period is "4-WEEKS" to database.
Ques 4 Rule:	IF not asked whether "MANAGER" THEN ask "MANAGER"? & add that asked "MAN-AGER" to database & attend to answer.
Class 5 Rule:	IF attribute "2-YEARS-SERVICE" THEN add that period is "4-WEEKS" to database.
Ques 5 Rule:	IF not asked whether "2-YEARS-SERVICE" THEN ask "2-YEARS-SERVICE"? & add that asked "2-YEARS-SERVICE" to database & attend to answer.
Class 6 Rule:	THEN add that period is "2-WEEKS" to database.

An examination of the rules will show that the program consists of several different types of rule. The predominant rules are those which examine the content of the database for employee attributes and, depending on the current content, either ask for further information or indicate the allowed holiday period. In addition, there is one rule (B) at the top of the set of rules which is used for attending to and acting upon the user's responses, and a rule (A) for passing on the solution to the user. It should further be noted that the rules vary in complexity, many of them having both multiple conditions and multiple actions. Indeed, there is even a rule (Class 6), required for the final guess on a negative path, which has no conditions; only the single action of declaring the period of "2-WEEKS".

Let us assume that the interpreter uses a simple control structure which executes the first rule for which the conditions match the facts in the database resulting in changes to the database. After a rule is executed, the flow of control is transferred to the top of the rule-set and the matching process begins again. Let us assume that the database is initially empty.

Cycle 1: The left-hand side (LHS) of none of the first fire rules matches the database. However, the LHS of Ques 2 does, since there is no record of the user being asked whether the employee is a "SENIOR-MANAGER". The system therefore responds to the action part of Ques 2 and asks whether he is a "SENIOR-MANAGER" then records in the database that the question has been asked and attends to the answer, which also gets recorded. In this instance the answer is "NO".

Cycle 2: The interpreter implementing the simple control structure given above now starts again to apply rules from the top. This time Ques 2 does not match since the fact that "SENIOR-MANAGER" has been asked is recorded in the database. The first rule to match this time is Ques 4, this setting off a similar cycle to that of the previous rule: the system asks whether the employee is a "MANAGER"; it records the asking of the question in the database; it attends to and records the answer – let us assume it is "YES".

Cycle 3: Given a positive response, Rule B fires. This rule deletes the item recording the positive response, and records in its place that one of the employee's attributes has been identified, namely that he is a "MANAGER".

Cycle 4: Ques 3 matches the contents of the database, the system asks whether the employee is a "GRADUATE" and gets the answer "NO".

Cycle 5: Class 5 is the first rule to fire. Obeying the action, the system asserts that "4-WEEKS" is the appropriate period and this is added to the database.

Cycle 6: Rule A can now fire since a period is recorded in the database. The system then prints the holiday period of "4-WEEKS".

The above program illustrates many of the basic features of production systems. However, as pointed out in Chapter 1, the level of complexity in the sample program is very quickly exceeded in a real application. For example, production rule based expert systems often use upwards of 800 rules, and it will be evident that with this number the control of execution may become a serious problem. One of the original attractions of production rule formalisms was their simplicity. Despite this ideal, it has been pointed out that in order to design usable systems significant deviations are necessary. These may involve introducing some structure into the database, having various levels of rule, and allowing rules to access standard programming procedures.

Finally, it should be noted that while production rules are the best known method of representing domain specific problem-solving knowledge there are others. For example, there are a number of systems which only represent the action portion of production rules and apply them as "operators" to transform some problem state to some other state. Such operators may be embedded within a variety of control structures, including conventional procedural programs. A further possibility, used notably in medical expert systems, is to organise problem-solving knowledge into static descriptions of diseases defined in terms of associated symptoms, the task of the diagnostic programs being to find the smallest set of diseases capable of causing a given set of symptoms (see the INTERNIST program in Chapter 6).

3.4   PROBLEMS OF CONTROL

The control structure in the previous example is a simple one, try the rules in descending order until one fires, then return to the top. In most real systems the problem of control is much more complex.

Problems of control within Artificial Intelligence are usually expressed with reference to the concept of what is termed a "state-space search". In knowledge-based problem-solving there is usually no single clear method of achieving a solution. It will thus be necessary to explore several possible paths, seeking to evaluate the possibility of success at each stage. The control structure of a problem-solving system defines the general strategy for selecting paths. One might even borrow the term "form" from logic and talk of a problem-solving "form" which may be applied to some specific problem in a particular domain.

The "state-space search" approach owes much to an early interest in automatic game-playing. In most games there are a finite number of positions (or "states") which may be reached under the fixed set of rules which define the play. It is therefore possible, in theory at least, to describe all possible sequences of play by enumerating all positions that may be attained from a given start position. This set of all possible positions may be represented as a tree, spreading from a root which is the start state for the game to a set of terminal positions at the end of the game. In Figure 3.14, for example, all possible positions are given for the first four moves of the simple game "noughts-and-crosses" (or "tic-tac-toe").

For those unfamiliar with the game, there are two types of token – "O" and "X" – and positions are defined with reference to a 3 by 3 matrix. One simple rule governs the placing of tokens, namely that the two

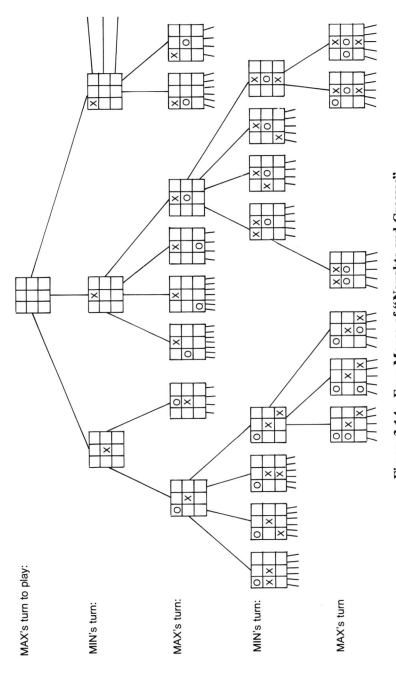

MAX's turn to play:

MIN's turn:

MAX's turn:

MIN's turn:

MAX's turn

Figure 3.14   Four Moves of "Noughts-and-Crosses"
(from Gloess P Y, 1981, *Understanding Artificial Intelligence*, Alfred Handy Guide, Alfred Publishing Co, Sherman Oaks, CA)

players (one playing "O" and one "X") take it in turns to put their respective token on any vacant cell in the matrix. The goal position is defined as a line of 3 "Os" or "Xs", the first player to attain such a line being the winner.

Within the "state-space" representation described above, patterns of tokens (states) that represent successful play may be sought among the terminal positions of the tree. A winning sequence of moves may be derived by generating a path from the start state to a winning state.

With a state-based representation of a problem space, it has been found fruitful to think of a solution as resulting from the application of rules or operators (representing the "actions" part of a rule) which are triggered by a given game state and produce a state transition.

In "noughts-and-crosses" there is only one trivial operator, namely the placing of a single token ("O" or "X") on an empty square in the matrix. However, with other games there may be several operators. For example, in chess the moves prescribed for each piece may be seen as operators which transform the patterns of chessmen on the board, so moving the game from state to state.

One problem remains. In a game of more complexity it will be necessary to provide some means of deciding which rule or operator to apply to which state in order to ensure progress towards the goal. It is the general strategy governing such decisions which is known as the control structure.

The simplest strategy would involve an exhaustive scan of the whole tree in order to identify appropriate moves. The direction in which the state space is reached is often significant in knowledge-based systems research.

In the state diagram in Figure 3.14, our start state is at the top of the figure and the goal states at the bottom. (There may be more than one start state in some state-spaces.) When such state diagrams are used in knowledge based systems, they are conventionally drawn the other way up, the goals being at the top and the start states at the bottom. This is because the focus of attention is on the goals (eg we want to reach a particular goal state, the solution to our problem). In such cases the search direction is still measured from the start state. For example, backward-chaining involves moving from goals to start state(s) and forward-chaining from start state(s) to goals. However, another way of expressing the search direction is either "top-down" or "bottom-up". In this case "top-down" refers to a search from goals to start state(s) and "bottom-up" a search from start state(s) to goals.

There is one more general point to make concerning the order of search through a state-space. Irrespective of the orientation of search, a tree of states originating from a given goal or start state may be examined either "depth-first" or "breadth-first". A "depth-first" search plunges deep into the tree from a given state, a sequence of successors to a state being considered until the path is exhausted, after which the next alternative path down the tree is explored in depth. On the other hand, a "breadth-first" search first generates all possible alternatives at a given level, then all alternatives at the next level, and so on. The search is thus conducted in breadth across the tree. Figure 3.15 illustrates this.

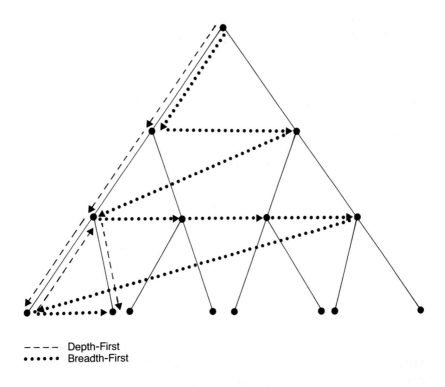

```
- - - -  Depth-First
● ● ● ● ● ●  Breadth-First
```

Figure 3.15   Depth- and Breadth-First Search

Irrespective of the order of search, there is still a potentially serious problem in trying to win a game (or solve a problem) by conducting an exhaustive search of the state-space. It may come as a surprise, but even with such a simple game as "noughts-and-crosses" there are 362,880 (9!) possible positions, although this does reduce to around 60,000 because of its many axes of symmetry. With a complex game such as chess it would not be possible to search the whole game tree. Haugeland has estimated that a five-move look-ahead gives a quadrillon (10^{15}) of possibilities, and forty moves (an average game) gives 10^{120} possibilities. He points out that there have been fewer than 10^{80} seconds since the beginning of the universe!! At each step, the number of choices multiplies the total number of combinations. This is termed a "combinatorial explosion", and rules out the strategy of exhaustive search for most real games, and also for most knowledge-based systems.

It is evident from the very large number of positions in even a simple game such as "noughts-and-crosses" that no player will ever conduct an exhaustive search before making a move. What a player *will* do is to apply certain strategic rules to determine which moves are most likely to be successful. This will, in most cases, considerably reduce the number of positions that need to be tried. However, there is a further problem. It is rarely possible to identify with absolute certainty which moves should be considered. Some moves may at first sight appear unlikely to succeed, although they may be very effective given a particular counter-move. In most games (and knowledge processing situations in general) it is often not possible to find rules which will guarantee success. However, it is frequently possible to find rules which will increase the chance of success. Such rules are termed "heuristics" and a search involving them is termed (not surprisingly) a "heuristic search". A heuristic normally needs access to information which tells it how well it is performing. This information is called from an "evaluation function". In noughts-and-crosses a simple evaluation function is used. A value (a number) is assigned to each possible next move, the higher the value, the better it is for one player. The lower it is, the better it is for the other player. This is called a MINIMAX procedure.

To illustrate the application of MINIMAX to "noughts-and-crosses" let us assume that there are two players, named MAX (playing "X") and MIN (playing "0"). Values for the moves available to them may be obtained by counting all lines open to each player and then subtracting one from the other.

Applied to the game position given in Figure 3.16, with MAX to play, a choice must be made from moves 1, 2, 3 and 4. These have the values 0, 0, 1, – 1 respectively and MAX would choose move 3 as it has the highest value for this round.

The game of "noughts-and-crosses" is amenable to the construction of a single evaluation function which reliably produces an optimum solution path. However, it is often very difficult, if not impossible, to find such well behaved functions for many real-world problems. One complication, for example, which was mentioned above with reference to chess, is that a less favourable move may have to be made at one point of a game in order to gain a later advantage. An evaluation function which only considers one level of move at a time would not be capable of suggesting such an action.

Much of the work on control structures in Artificial Intelligence has been devoted to coping with these complex situations. Two general

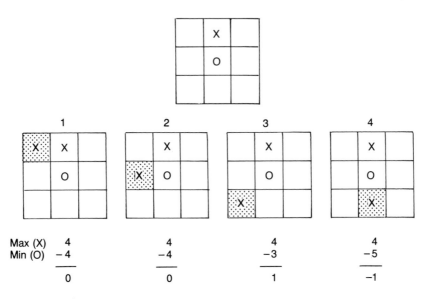

Figure 3.16   The Application of a "Noughts-and-Crosses" Evaluation Function

strategies applied with notable success in expert systems are:

i) to organise the problem space in such a way that it is possible early in the solution to tell whether it is likely to be successful, in which case the need to search a whole set of paths may be avoided;

ii) to organise the problem space into a number of sub-spaces having little, or no interaction between them. Each sub-problem may thus be solved without affecting the solution of successive problems.

Further discussion of these strategies will not be developed at this point but will be left until the relevant expert systems are discussed (in Chapters 7 and 8 respectively). This is because the applicability of different control strategies depends very much upon the structure of domain knowledge and is thus best considered within the context of a specific problem. Indeed, the process of designing knowledge-based systems can be seen as an exercise in identifying those features of the domain which will enable the problem to be so organised as to minimise computation. Part II, dealing with individual systems, has been approached with this principle in mind.

Part II

Examples of Expert Systems

4 Expert Systems and Expert Problem-Solvers

4.1 KNOWLEDGE-BASED PROBLEM-SOLVING

In Part 1 we discussed a number of programming concepts and techniques which are used in the design and implementation of intelligent knowledge-based systems. Many of these were developed within the discipline of Artificial Intelligence and were in response to the switch in focus towards domain-dependent control structures. This amounted to a change from the objective of finding a few powerful general-purpose problem-solving methods, to that of mechanising the domain knowledge actually used by human experts to solve complex problems.

The project which pioneered this change was DENDRAL (see Chapter 7). The DENDRAL research group was established in Stanford University in 1965 to work on the design of a system to help chemists infer the structure of chemical compounds from mass spectral data. The system – Heuristic DENDRAL – was seminal in that it successfully made use of explicit expert knowledge of mass spectrometry and so demonstrated the potential of the young discipline of Artificial Intelligence to undertake problem-solving in complex, real-world domains.

The incorporation of explicit domain knowledge into problem-solving programs proved to be of great practical and theoretical importance. First, it enabled Artificial Intelligence to solve real-world problems which were previously beyond its powers. From this initial exploration of "knowledge programming" a whole tradition has developed, covering such diverse areas of application as teaching systems, natural language understanding and diagnostic problem-solving. Secondly, the knowledge-based approach generated its own questions which had the effect of extending the theoretical interests of the subject, raising not only issues of knowledge representation (Chapter 3) but also questions concerning the structure of the different cognitive functions which programs were required to simulate (eg story understanding, question answering, fault finding).

Although knowledge programming has emerged since 1965 as being important for a very wide range of applications, the approach has continued to be most successful for problem-solving in areas requiring a rich body of personal expertise. Computer systems which mechanise such expertise have become generally known as "expert systems".

There are now a substantial number of "expert systems" which can claim expert, or near expert, performance in a wide range of domains, undertaking such problem-solving tasks as medical diagnosis, data analysis and planning. Some of the best known systems are discussed in the following chapters. These include:

— MYCIN, a system for diagnosing bacterial infections (Chapter 5);

— PROSPECTOR, a system for aiding the evaluation of geological prospects (Chapter 5);

— INTERNIST, an advisor on general internal medicine (Chapter 6);

— CASNET, a system for diagnosing the eye disease glaucoma (Chapter 6);

— Heuristic DENDRAL and Meta-DENDRAL, systems for inferring the structure of chemical compounds (Chapter 7);

— R1, a system for configuring VAX computers (Chapter 8);

— MOLGEN, a system to assist in the design of genetics experiments (Chapter 8).

Eighteen years have elapsed since the initiation of DENDRAL, and one might expect the development of a clear set of general principles for designing expert systems. However, the principles which have emerged are far from general, representing little more than a summation of conventional wisdom. The first part of this book has been directed towards providing a foundation for understanding these principles so that the reader can appreciate the strength (and limitations) of current expert systems techniques. The main points of the conventional wisdom are noted by Davis, a prominent worker in the area, as:

— separate the inference engine from the knowledge base;

— use as uniform a representation as possible, the preferred form of representation being production rules;

— keep the inference engine (control structure) simple;

— provide some form of facility by which the system can explain its conclusions to the user;

— favour problems that require the use of substantial bodies of empirical associative knowledge over those that may be solved using causal or mathematical knowledge.

The above principles provided a powerful starting point for expert systems design. The rule-based representation discussed in Part 1, for example, permits knowledge to be added freely as the system evolves and places few restrictions on content. It is thus possible for knowledge which is understood at a "deep", theoretical level to be combined with items based on no more than "rule of thumb" ideas to produce an effective expert system. The use of a relatively simple control structure also has advantages. Apart from reducing the overall complexity, the choice of a straightforward deductive mechanism in many systems makes it relatively easy to implement an "explanation facility" by which the expert problem-solver can explain its reasoning to the user. Such facilities have been found to make an expert system more acceptable by making its reasoning less opaque and by aiding the modification and debugging of the knowledge base.

All of the expert systems to be discussed in this section focus upon some narrow and relatively well defined subject area. The identification of such a focus for work is one of a number of general criteria for existing techniques. A number have been given by the DENDRAL group. They are quoted in full.

"—Focus on a narrow speciality area that does not involve a lot of common sense knowledge."

Artificial Intelligence techniques have not progressed to the point where computers are adept at common-sense reasoning. Building a system with expertise in several domains is extremely difficult, since this is likely to involve different paradigms and formalisms.

"—Select a task that is neither too easy or too difficult for human experts."

Based on current techniques "too easy" might be defined as "taking a few minutes"; "too hard" might be defined as "requiring a few hours". Hopefully, our abilities to build expert systems will grow, but for now these rules of thumb are probably right. Don't aim for a program that is an expert in domain D; rather aim for an expert performing task T within domain D. The number of relative concepts should be bounded and of the order of many hundred.

"—Define the task clearly."

This is both obvious and crucial. At the outset, the designer should be able to describe the nature of the inputs and outputs rather precisely, and the expert should be able to specify many of the important concepts and relations. The designer should have access to many specific examples of problems and solutions.

"—Commitment from an articulate expert is essential."

After all, knowledge engineering is a process of rendering human expertise into machine-usable form. This cannot be done unless there is a long-term commitment from such an expert.

All of the systems we describe follow these principles and owe a considerable measure of their success to them.

There are two further criteria for task selection, both of which are implied by the above points. First, it is a distinct advantage if the subject area has already been formalised to some degree. This was true of the knowledge required for interpreting mass spectra used by DENDRAL, for example, where manuals written to guide interpretation already existed. Another example is the detailed causal models of the disease of the eye – "glaucoma" – which are used in the system CASNET. Even though one of the most publicised features of expert systems is that they enable automated expert reasoning to be achieved in areas lacking a formal theoretical foundation – ie by using rules to encode empirical associations – it is an advantage to have some measure of formal structure available to guide the organising of associations in the system.

A second criterion is to select domains which are amenable to verbal expression. A key test for this is to imagine that the interaction with the system is to take place over the telephone. This rule will eliminate those areas in which knowledge is either predominantly sensory or is "tacit". The restriction regarding sensory knowledge would eliminate such topics as tea blending and wine tasting as suitable areas for expert systems, it being difficult to describe the relevant objects and relations in a manner which would be understood by anyone but the expert providing the knowledge. The restriction regarding "tacit"knowledge applies naturally in areas which are essentially practical (engineering skills, for example). Here the practitioner is usually unable to provide the facts and theoretical principles underlying his performance, hence the user of the expert system is denied any rationale for questions or instructions.

4.2 A CLASSIFICATION SCHEME FOR EXPERT SYSTEMS

A report by Stefik and his colleagues presents a scheme for classifying expert systems. This scheme is comprehensive and organises systems in terms of the degree to which they are capable of undertaking problems which are not "well structured". The term "well structured" has been used in this context to describe a problem which is ideally suited to efficient automatic solution. Given the state-space representation of problems discussed in the final section of Chapter 3, this means that:

i)   the search space must be small;

ii)   domain knowledge must be reliable (it must not contain error and must be consistent);

iii)   the data provided by the user must be reliable and static over time (the data relevant to a solution must not become invalid as the solution proceeds).

Stefik presents a number of advantages following from these three principles. First, with a small search space there will be no need to use complex control strategies to enable programs to run within the resources of the machine. A problem solution could be obtained by conducting a simple exhaustive search of the space without having to be concerned with combinatorial explosions or with the need to select the most efficient representation for domain knowledge (which will not necessarily be the most transparent).

The advantage of reliable knowledge and data follows from the discussion of logical inference in Chapter 2. If knowledge and data are reliable it should never be necessary to revise a solution given additional information. The solution should proceed "monotonically" with conclusions adding to each other as new information becomes available. Moreover, the solution will be both definite and correct; a conclusion will never be in any sense approximate and will never be false. Finally, Stefik points out that static data provides the additional advantage that conclusions relying upon some given data item will remain true throughout the solution, ie the validity of the data will not change with time, such changes requiring the re-computation of conclusions using that data items.

It is our opinion that Stefik's classification scheme provides a useful method of introducing order into the potentially confusing mixture of data structures and processing techniques used in expert systems. We have therefore decided to follow it in principle for selecting and organising systems for discussion.

The next four chapters discuss a selection of expert systems which illustrate some major problems in building knowledge-based problem-solvers and the techniques which have been used to overcome them. The focus is upon the predominant characteristics of the problem-solving required to undertake a particular task in a particular domain, and the Artificial Intelligence programming techniques used to implement them.

Many of these techniques are interesting in that they have largely evolved as a direct result of expert systems research. Moreover, the area is still developing. One of the lessons of expert systems research is that even slight changes in domain or task often produce sufficient novel characteristics to render formerly effective techniques inapplicable. Hence, it is frequently necessary to engage to some degree in fundamental research in addition to application engineering. However, it is to be hoped that the material presented in the following chapters will provide a basis for understanding the problems involved in engineering knowledge and the techniques of implementation.

4.2.1 Rule-Based Diagnostic Systems for Reasoning from Uncertain Data and Knowledge (Chapter 5)

The two principal rule-based diagnostic systems to be discussed are MYCIN and PROSPECTOR. These systems were early developments but were sufficiently impressive both in the level of expert reasoning accomplished and their simplicity of construction that they encouraged others.

The problems addressed by these systems are largely those of indefinite knowledge and imprecise data, rather than those of managing the problem space. Given careful definition of the diagnostic domain, the search space may be kept acceptably small. Hence, it is possible to traverse it using the simple technique of problem reduction: the problem of "proving" a given solution is reduced to that of proving a set of simpler problems. The handling of unreliable data and knowledge is achieved through some form of weighted evaluation.

4.2.2 Associative and Causal Approaches to Diagnosis (Chapter 6)

Neither MYCIN nor PROSPECTOR make any claim to model the actual diagnostic strategies used by experts. Moreover, their strength lies in their ability to reason effectively without recourse to causal or theoretical knowledge, the ability to reason from "first principles" being an important feature of human expert performance.

The first system (INTERNIST) to be discussed in Chapter 6 seeks to model the reasoning of medical clinicians and also to give accurate diagnosis in complex situations where more than one disease is present. Both these objectives are tackled using an associative network representation, diseases being related to symptoms which indicate them by different types of associative link. The task of the processor is first to identify a set of diseases as competing candidates for causing the symptoms and then to employ some strategy which is dependent upon the number of candidates in order to decide between them.

The second system (CASNET) addresses the problem of making a diagnosis in an area where there is considerable knowledge of the causal motivation of the disease. Here it is possible to provide a system that not only verifies that the given disease is present, but also predicts the progress of the disease over time and provides a record of treatment. To achieve this, CASNET represents a disease not as a static state but as a dynamic process that can be modelled as a network of causally linked pathophysiological states. The system conducts a diagnosis by determining a pattern of pathological causal pathways present in the patient and identifying the pattern with a disease category.

4.2.3 Reducing Large Search Spaces Through Factoring (Chapter 7)

This approach attacks the difficulties arising from the size of the problem space. This was first faced early on in the history of expert systems in the DENDRAL project. The principal solution was to employ the "generate-and-test" technique in which selected states are developed, generating a solution tree to a certain depth. Heuristic tests are then applied to the tree and a decision made as to whether to continue to elaborate the branch or to prune it away, so halting further propagation.

The success of the "generate-and-test" technique is very dependent upon the factoriability of the state-space, and thus the ability to predict early in the development of the problem tree which branches will lead to solutions. For many problems, it may be necessary to develop the tree to a considerable depth before it is safe to rule out a path; a path which is initially unpromising may later yield a viable solution. With "generate-and-test" one either prunes early and risks missing solutions, or leaves pruning to later, in which case there may be no significant saving in processing. It would be only a little more expensive to conduct an exhaustive search. It turns out that the chemical structures handled by DENDRAL offer the appropriate constraints to make early pruning a viable strategy.

4.2.4 Handling Large Search Spaces Through Abstraction (Chapter 8)

In many expert systems applications it may not be necessary to identify all solutions and to choose the best, but be sufficient to find a single solution. These applications may often be approached by reasoning with abstractions concerning the structure of the problem space. In this way it is often possible to avoid a combinatorial explosion without early pruning. Chapter 8 gives examples of the use of different types of abstraction and of systems that employ them.

First we discuss the very successful commercially implemented program, called R1, employed to configure VAX computers. This system is rule-based and contains fixed abstractions concerning the problem space in the form of meta-rules. However, this approach requires that all of the information needed for testing a partial solution be available at one time. With other problem domains this cannot always be guaranteed.

An alternative discussed by Stefik is used with considerable success in MOLGEN. This employs a principle of "least commitment" which states that decisions should be postponed until there is enough information. Stefik argues that "This approach tends to exploit the synergy of interactions between subproblems. It requires the ability to suspend activity in subproblems, move information between subproblems, and then restart them as information becomes available. In this case the problem-solving knowledge is much richer than in previous methods".

5 The Handling of Uncertain Evidence – MYCIN and PROSPECTOR

5.1 INTRODUCTION

The two expert systems described in this chapter operate on well-organised knowledge bases – infectious disease knowledge (MYCIN) and geological models (PROSPECTOR). However, in both applications the knowledge is often inexact so the systems need to use a form of plausible reasoning. At the heart of both systems therefore are techniques for expressing measures of belief, that is, the "suggestiveness" or otherwise of evidence in favour of a given conclusion. MYCIN uses a set of belief measures called "certainty factors" influenced by the theory of confirmation. PROSPECTOR uses conditional probabilities and Bayes' Theorem.

Both systems have been designed with relatively simple control structures. The architecture is based upon the production system approach and consists of:

(a)   a collection of facts;

(b)   a set of production rules;

(c)   an inference engine which is either forward chained, backward chained (or both), together with a knowledge structure which enables the control structure to decide which candidate rules should take part in the inference mechanism;

(d)   a mechanism for drawing inference from uncertain or incomplete evidence.

The systems differ mainly in the way in which points (c) and (d) are implemented. In MYCIN, groupings of rules within a particular context are defined at generation time. In PROSPECTOR, the rules are described in terms of a network in which the set of rules to be considered are those defined by the exit (or entry) arcs of a node. The inference engine in each case provides goal-directed searching (in which a rule is normally used to derive more information about its premises) or data-directed searching (in which a rule is used to cause alterations to the database via its action part). Whilst both systems allow an intermixing of the two modes, the systems tend to be mainly backward chained.

The existence of the domain-dependent control structure necessarily means that the systems are highly domain-dependent. However, in both cases attempts have been made to apply the approach to other knowledge areas with similar characteristics. Indeed, the domain-independent parts of MYCIN have been extracted to form "empty" MYCIN or EMYCIN which has successfully been applied to a number of similar domains, eg PUFF (respiratory intensive care), SACOM (engineering structure calculations), GRAVIDA (pregnancy advice), CLOT (blood disorders) and VM (ventilation management). The PROSPECTOR approach has been used in water resource management (HYDRO) and has been implemented as a number of "empty" expert systems (SAGE, MICRO-EXPERT). In all these cases however the knowledge domain must be capable of being cast into MYCIN- or PROSPECTOR-like representations.

The MYCIN approach has been modified to cope with time-dependent aspects (which exist for example in the management of cancer therapy). The resultant system is known as ONCOCIN.

5.2 MYCIN (EMYCIN) OVERVIEW

MYCIN was developed at Stanford University to assist physicians with advice on diagnosis and treatment of infectious diseases. Its goals are therefore concerned with the identification of the offending organism and with the treatment of the disease.

5.2.1 Facts

Facts are stored as triples in the form CONTEXT-PARAMETER-VALUE. A context is some real-world entity such as a patient. A parameter is an attribute of the context (eg age) and the value is an instance of the parameter (eg 25 years). With each fact triple is associated a certainty factor (CF) with a value between -1 (negation) and $+1$ (certainty). An example would be

ORGANISM1 – IDENTITY – PSEUDOMONAS .8

meaning "The identity of the organism 1 is pseudomonas with a certainty factor of .8"

At the beginning of a consultation there will be many such triples, some of which will be incomplete. Certain triples represent the goals of the consultation and these will obviously be unfilled at the start.

5.2.2 Production Rules

Reasoning about the knowledge domain is achieved by encoding expert knowledge as a set of production rules of the form

IF premise THEN action (CF)

where the premise is some conjunction of triples and the action usually involves the instantiation of a triple. The certainty factor CF of the rule is used in conjunction with the CFs of the relevant triples to calculate new certainty factors for the action triple. A rule can be applied either:

(a) from known premises to instantiate action triples (forward chaining, data-driven);

(b) from a known action triple to determine what premise triples need to be determined (backward chaining, goal-directed).

In MYCIN, rules are defined to be either forward or backward chained. The rules are repeatedly applied, domain-dependent knowledge being used to decide which rules to consider, until the goal triple(s) is instantiated. In some cases rules will instantiate triples by questioning the physician.

An example of a MYCIN rule is:

IF   1)   It is not known whether the organism was able to grow aerobically

AND   2)   The site of the culture is blood

OR   The lab has attempted to grow the organism anaerobically

AND   3)   The organism was able to grow anaerobically

THEN   There is evidence that the aerobicity of the organism is facul (.5) or anaerobic (.2).

This would be written in LISP as

premise: ($AND (NOTKNOWN CNTXT AIRGROW)
($OR (SAME CNTXT SITE BLOOD)
(SAME CNTXT ANTRY))
(SAME CNTXT ANGROW))
action: (CONCLUDE* CNTXT AIR TALLY '((FACUL
500) (ANAEROBIC 200)))

The premise of a rule has the general form

($AND clause 1 clause 2 clause 3 . . .)

The premise is TRUE if and only if all its constituent clauses are TRUE. The individual clauses take the form

(predicate-function-name   list-of-arguments)

If any clause is FALSE the rule is rejected. CNTXT is a variable. Whenever the rule is used it substitutes the name of a relevant context. This name is derived using other knowledge.

The predicate functions (eg SAME) return a truth value when applied to a triple. The truth value, depending upon the function, will be true, false, or a certainty factor. For example, SAME returns FALSE if the certainty factor is $<.2$ or the value of the certainty factor if it is $>.2$. KNOWN returns a value TRUE if the certainty factor is $>.2$ and FALSE if it is $<.2$. DEFINITE returns a value of TRUE only if the certainty factor is 1.

5.2.3 Certainty Factor Calculations

The CONCLUDE predicate adds a triple to the database with a computed certainty factor. This factor is computed from the certainty factor of the premise, the certainty factor of the rule and the triple's original certainty factor if it existed already.

Firstly the certainty factor of the premise is computed as the minimum of its clauses. This is then multiplied by the certainty factor of the rule (in the action part) to give a certainty factor CR. If the triple did not exist previously then CR would be allocated as its certainty factor. If however it already existed with a certainty factor of CI, the new certainty factor CF is calculated as follows.

$$CF = CI + CR(1 - CI) \qquad\qquad CR, CI > 0$$

$$CF = -(|CI| + |CR|(1-|CI|)) \qquad CR,CI<0$$

$$CF = \frac{CI + CR}{1 - \min(|CI|,|CR|)} \qquad CI.CR<0$$

Combination of 1 and −1 is defined to be 1.

This certainty factor approach allows the system to cope with judgmental reasoning. It was designed to be natural to and easily understandable by experts who contributed to the database and the users of the system.

The variation in the computed CF is shown in Figure 5.1.

The developers of MYCIN have been reasonably satisfied with this approach. They regard it as "a first step towards the development of a coherent theory for the management of uncertainty in complex reasoning situations".

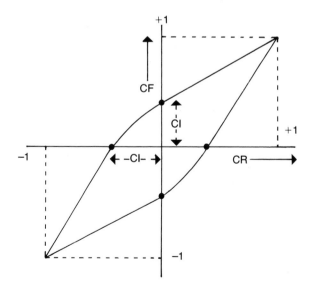

Figure 5.1   Certainty Factor Interpolation

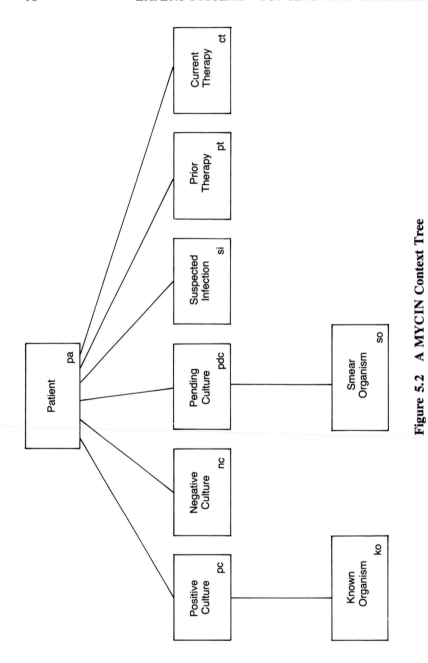

Figure 5.2 A MYCIN Context Tree

5.2.4   Domain-Dependent Control Structure

The control structure consists of an inference engine for forward or backward chaining together with a knowledge structure which enables the system to decide which rules to try next. The ordering of the rules is not significant. All relevant rules are applied until one particular rule concludes a goal with certainty, in which case the rest of the rules are ignored. The relevance of a rule is defined by the domain-dependent control structure. MYCIN mainly uses backward chaining, though a few rules are defined to be applied in forward chaining mode only.

The domain-dependent control knowledge is stored as a context tree. This tree organises the triples in the knowledge base into a hierarchy and is used to direct the flow of the consultation. The root of the tree is the starting point for the selection of initial goals which the system will attempt to satisfy. The tree is a hierarchy of context types (or templates), and the actual triples which exist or are created during the consultation form a structure which mimics the context tree. A rule always refers to a context type and rules are grouped together into rulegroups defined by a set of applicable context types. All rules which belong to a rulegroup which refers to a context of interest are considered for firing. A MYCIN context tree is illustrated in Figure 5.2, and a particular instance of the context tree is shown in Figure 5.3.

The context tree, by defining hierarchical relationships between contexts and parameter groupings, thus steers the rule interpreter during the consultation. Furthermore, since the context tree reflects the relationship of objects in the domain it helps to provide a consultation system which is familiar to the user.

5.2.5   Obtaining Information from the User

Because of the nature of the stored knowledge, the sequence of questions asked of the user physician will depend upon current instantiations in the data base. Questions are asked either when the rules fail, in order to determine necessary information, or when the information is defined as having to come from the user (ie laboratory data). The designer has some control over the manner in which information is elicited. A question can be elaborated if it is not understood, allowing different sets of questions for experienced and inexperienced users. An ASKFIRST property tells the system always to endeavour to find out the value of a parameter from the user first.

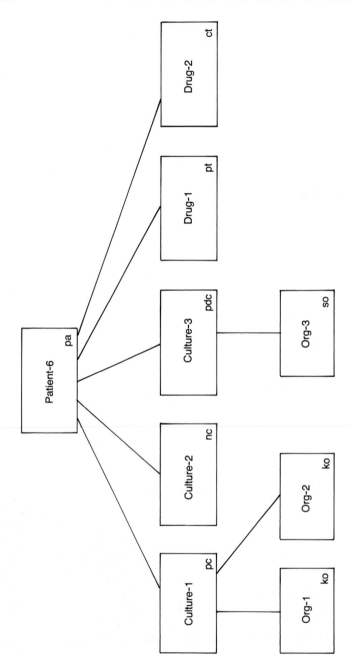

Figure 5.3   A MYCIN Instance Tree

(from van Melle W, Scott A C, Bennett J S and Peairs M, *The EMYCIN Manual*, Stanford University Report No. STAN-CS-81-885, October 1981, p 18)

The way in which an expert system elicits information from the user contributes (or otherwise) to its acceptability. The system designer has to provide an acceptable user interface. This aspect of MYCIN was not wholly satisfactory and a different approach was used when the ONCO-CIN system was developed.

5.2.6 Explanation Facilities

When a system is used to advise physicians on patient treatment, the user physician must have confidence that it is providing a properly reasoned consultation. MYCIN therefore (like many other expert systems) has a facility for explaining and justifying its performance. Such a facility is also useful in educational situations. At any time a user may question the system as to HOW or WHY it reached a decision. The provision of such "explanations" is simplified by exploiting the rule-based architecture.

When asked WHY, MYCIN first lists the action part of the rule. It then lists the premises already instantiated and finally the premises which are required to be instantiated by the question. Repeated use of WHY is interpreted as a request for display of the next rule in the current reasoning chain. HOW acts in the opposite direction.

Whilst the questioning facility in MYCIN is quite powerful, it is limited to reasoning about the immediate vicinity of the MYCIN reasoning state during the consultation. Furthermore there are many knowledge aspects which MYCIN knows nothing about, eg WHY is Pseudomonas a bacterium? It has no explicit causal knowledge of the domain of interest.

5.2.7 Extensions to the MYCIN Approach – TEIRESIAS and GUIDON

A system such as MYCIN is built up as a result of a series of consultations between the builders of the system and experts in the knowledge domain of interest. This process is very labour intensive and error prone. Experts generally know more than they think they know and cannot always easily express their reasoning processes. Knowledge elicitation – that is obtaining from experts the knowledge to be used in building an expert system – is generally recognised to be a time-consuming and difficult process. The objective of TEIRESIAS was to reduce the role of the system builder in this process by allowing the domain expert to interact directly with the system. The system chosen was MYCIN but the ideas and techniques of TEIRESIAS could be used in a wider context. The system is also illustrative of the meta-rule concept which has been briefly alluded to earlier.

The system is concerned with three key issues – comprehensibility, debugging and knowledge elicitation. Comprehensibility is concerned with providing a system in which the end user can understand what is going on in his own terms. Debugging is a serious problem in expert system construction. What do we do when an expert disagrees with a conclusion of our system? The problems of knowledge elicitation have already been briefly discussed, but it includes not only the initial building of the system but also covers the addition or modification of knowledge at a later stage.

TEIRESIAS provides explanations to the user of how results have been obtained and the motivation for conclusions and advice. Once acceptable conclusions have been achieved the user can debug the knowledge base by querying results and demanding explanations. Then he can use the knowledge transfer facilities to add to or alter knowledge in the database. In order to perform these functions TEIRESIAS requires more knowledge than MYCIN – knowledge about itself. This knowledge is represented by an additional set of rules, called meta-rules, containing knowledge about how it reasons and how much it knows. Using this additional knowledge it provides an explanation by recapitulating the program's actions in reaching a particular goal. An example of a meta-rule is

IF   (1) the infection is a pelvic-abscess

       (2) there are rules that mention in their premises Enterobacteriaceae

       (3) there are rules that mention in their premises gram positive rods

THEN   there is suggestive evidence (.4) that rules dealing with Enterobacteriaceae should be invoked before those dealing with gram positive rods.

In other words try rules about Enterobacteriaceae before rules about gram positive rods because Enterobacteriaceae are normally associated with pelvic-abscesses.

The system also has "rule models" which are abstract descriptions of subsets of rules which have characteristics in common. It therefore has expectations about rules and will check with the user if its expectations are not realised. These rule models are related to the frame concepts discussed in Chapter 3. The models are organised into a tree and TEIRESIAS starts at the top descending until it finds the closest fit. The system also has additional natural language facilities (essentially keyword based) which improve the interaction with the user.

GUIDON was developed to use the explanation facilities of MYCIN for teaching purposes. To do this it has teaching knowledge which is additional to the MYCIN knowledge base and is encoded in over 200 tutorial rules. In theory the system is not totally dependent on MYCIN, and its rules could be replaced with diagnostic rules from another domain. The additional knowledge guides the tutorial, constructs a student model and responds to initiatives from the student. An example of a tutorial rule (in fact a meta-rule) is

IF (1) There are rules which have a bearing on this goal which have succeeded but have not been discussed
(2) The number of rules which have a bearing on this goal which have succeeded is 1
(3) There is strong evidence that the student has applied this rule

THEN Simply state the rule and its conclusion.

The dialogue allows the student to take the initiative when appropriate, ie switching topics, referring to earlier topics, etc, so that he guides the interaction. The system compares MYCIN's solution of the problem with the student's attempt, which may only be a partial solution. A weakness of the approach is the reliance on MYCIN's rules. Thus if the student's reasoning is based upon different concepts than those of MYCIN or he is using incorrect rules, the system does not perform satisfactorily.

5.3 PROSPECTOR OVERVIEW

PROSPECTOR was developed to assist field geologists. It was designed to provide three major types of advice – the evaluation of sites for the existence of certain deposits, the evaluation of geological resources in a region, and the selection of the most favourable drilling sites. The program was developed by SRI International in association with geological consultants and the U.S. Geological Survey.

Expert geologists apply highly specific models when identifying likely sites for ore deposits. In PROSPECTOR these models are coded into a computer system and systematically interpreted to give site evaluation advice. One key feature of the geological expert knowledge is that it is

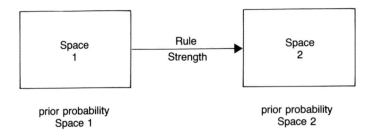

Figure 5.4   PROSPECTOR Model Detail

incomplete and uncertain. Special techniques are again used to cope with this but in a different way than the MYCIN certainty factor approach.

5.3.1   Geological Models

As with MYCIN the basic knowledge of the geological expert is stored as a set of facts and rules. The basic idea is the same but because of the way PROSPECTOR knowledge is constructed it is not convenient to talk about them separately. A model (15 are mentioned in the final report) consists of spaces connected by rules. A space may be some observable evidence or a hypothesis and each space has a probability value indicating how true it is. At the beginning of the run these probabilities are usually low. Rules specify how a change in the probability of one space affects another. This is illustrated in Figure 5.4.

Thus if the prior probability of Space 1 is altered, the rule propagates the effect to Space 2.

The similarity to MYCIN is obvious. Space 1 corresponds to a "premise" and Space 2 to an "action". A model is built up by connecting spaces with rules in the form of a network. Note that in the network rules may be ANDed, ORed or NOTed. Each time a space prior probability is altered, its effect is propagated through the network. An example of a PROSPECTOR network (part of a model) is given in Figure 5.5.

In the diagram each space is labelled with its prior probability and the rules have two factors which determine their strength – a sufficiency factor and a necessity factor.

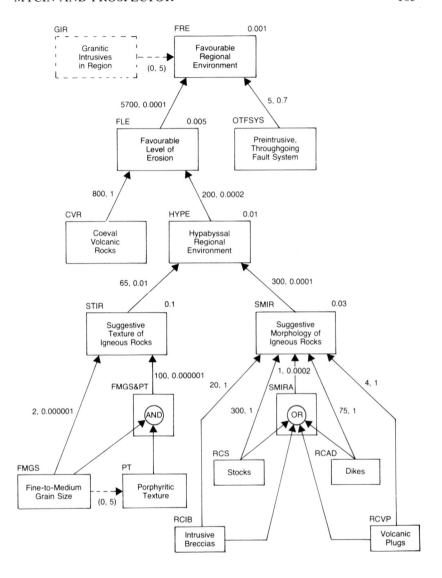

Figure 5.5   A Part of a PROSPECTOR Model
(from Reboh R, *Knowledge Engineering Techniques and Tools in the PROSPECTOR Environment*, Technical Note No. 243, June 1981, SRI International, Menlo Park, California, p 15)

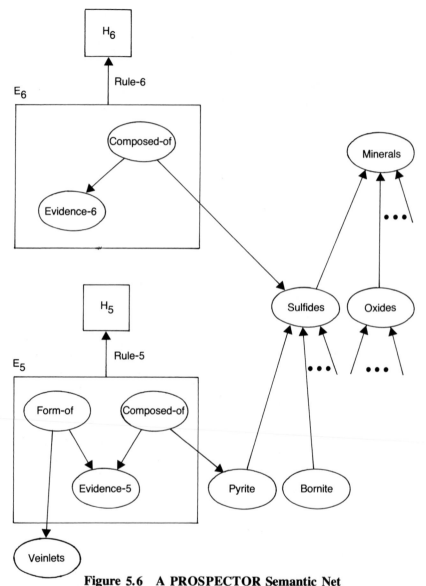

Figure 5.6   A PROSPECTOR Semantic Net
(from Duda R O, Hart P E, Barrett P, Gaschnig J G, Kolonige K, Reboh
R and Slocum J, *Development of the PROSPECTOR Consultation System
for Mineral Exploration*, Final Report, October 1978, SRI International,
Menlo Park, California, p 21)

The differences from MYCIN should also be clear. The whole model deals with probabilities of existing spaces. We do not create spaces or instantiate them, only change their probabilities as evidence is collected. The spaces at the base of the model elicit information from the user.

The inference network described above has no understanding of the context of the rules and the geological relationships of the spaces. A simple example is taken from one of the PROSPECTOR reports. One rule states

IF pyrite in veinlets is present THEN . . .

Another states

IF sulfides are present THEN . . .

In fact a pyrite is a sulfide so that a user response to the first rule implies a response to the second. A simple keyword scan for the word "pyrite" which associates it with "sulfide" will not suffice, since statements such as "has the same colour as pyrite" would be incorrectly interpreted. PROS-PECTOR solves this problem by storing a taxonomy of minerals as a semantic network (see Chapter 3). Figure 5.6 illustrates the concept.

In Figure 5.6, the square boxes represent spaces in the inference net. The semantic network is shown as connections between oval boxes. Each space can have an internal structure and may be connected to an external one. The additional semantic network enables the system to deduce that pyrite is a member of the sulfide group.

In PROSPECTOR therefore we have a semantic network of nodes and arcs which is further partitioned into higher level spaces which form the nodes of the inference network. Nodes which are unique to a space are included within the space and nodes which can be referred to by other statements appear outside. This is illustrated by the PROSPECTOR representations of

"A rhyolite plug is present"

in Figure 5.7.

5.3.2 Control Mechanism

The control mechanism supports a mixed-initiative interaction. The user can take control at any time using certain commands. In other words he need not always answer a PROSPECTOR question. Early in the consul-

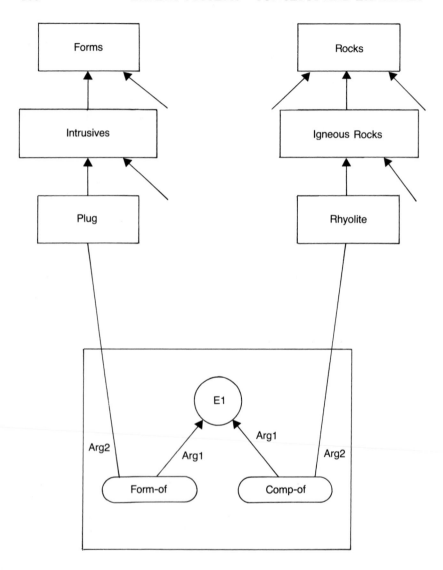

Figure 5.7   Internal and External Nodes
(from Reboh R, *Knowledge Engineering Techniques and Tools in the PROSPECTOR Environment*, Technical Note No. 243, June 1981, SRI International, Menlo Park, California, p 11)

tation for example, the user can influence the choice of the initial hypothesis through volunteering observations or can ask PROSPEC-TOR to investigate a particular hypothesis.

When PROSPECTOR is in control it decides which hypothesis to work on, and uses a depth-first strategy for traversing the inference net. Where there is a choice of rules to pursue it will select the one with the greatest potential for increasing the odds on the hypothesis (or ruling it out). Techniques are used to minimise ineffective questioning. At any time a user can ask for a question to be rephrased or ask PROSPECTOR to explain its reasons for asking a particular question. He can also demand an explanation of the current state of evaluation of the prospect.

Rules can be employed in either data-driven or goal-directed modes.

5.3.3 Relationships and Uncertainty

In PROSPECTOR there are three types of relationship between spaces:

a) a rule strength between spaces using necessity and sufficiency factors;

b) logical relationships indicating how combinations of assertions will be handled (AND, OR, NOT);

c) contextual relationships indicating an ordering of assertion determination.

5.3.3.1 The Necessity and Sufficiency Factors

We have already pointed out that each rule has a "rule strength" associated with it, which measures the degree to which a change in probability of one space will affect the probability of another. The source space (assertion) and the target space (hypothesis) are related by this rule strength which is described by two numbers, LS and LN. To describe what LS and LN are we will use an example. Let us assert that

"IF it snows THEN it is cold"
or   IF (E) THEN (H)

In this example we could measure weather conditions over a lengthy period then we could work out

condition	*probability*
snow and cold	SC
snow and not cold	SNC
no snow and cold	NSC
no snow and not cold	NSNC

Of course SC + SNC + NSC + NSNC = 1.

From this we can work out some probabilities using the notation $P(H|E)$ to represent the probability of H when we know E is true.

So

$$P(snow) = SC + SNC$$
$$P(cold) = SC + NSC$$
$$P(cold|snow) = SC/(SC + SNC)$$
$$P(snow|cold) = SC/(SC + NSC)$$

Combining these

$$\frac{SC}{(SC + SNC)} = \frac{SC}{(SC + NSC)} \cdot \frac{(SC + NSC)}{(SC + SNC)}$$

or

$$P(cold|snow) = P(snow|cold) \cdot \frac{P(cold)}{P(snow)}$$

more generally

$$P(H|E) = P(E|H) \cdot \frac{P(H)}{P(E)}$$

which is Bayes' Theorem.

Equally we can derive

$$P(\sim H|E) = P(E|\sim H) \cdot \frac{P(\sim H)}{P(E)}$$

where

$$P(\sim H) = 1 - P(H) \qquad (ie\ NOT\ P(H))$$

Dividing gives

$$\frac{P(H|E)}{P(\sim H|E)} = \frac{P(E|H)}{P(E|\sim H)} \cdot \frac{P(H)}{P(\sim H)}$$

But odds $= \dfrac{\text{Probability}}{1 - \text{Probability}}$

Therefore $O(H|E) = \dfrac{P(E|H)}{P(E|{\sim}H)} \cdot O(H)$

or $\qquad O(H|E) = LS.O(H)$

which is the odds version of Bayes' Theorem and tells us how the odds of H change with an observed true E. LS is called the "sufficiency factor".

One can equally follow through an analogous derivation for

$$O(H|{\sim}E) = LN.O(H)$$

Given that E is definitely untrue this tells us how to calculate the new odds of H. LN is called the "necessity factor".

In our earlier snow/cold example

$$LS = \frac{SC/(SC+NSC)}{SNC/(SNC+NSNC)} \qquad LN = \frac{NSC/(NSC+SC)}{NSNC/(NSNC+SNC)}$$

LS and LN are related by the equation

$$LN = (1-LS.P(E|H)/(1-P(E|{\sim}H)))$$

In our example

$$LS = \frac{SC \cdot NSNC}{SNC \cdot NSC} \, LN$$

And it can easily be shown generally that if

LS $>$ 1 then LN $<$ 1
LS $<$ 1 then LN $>$ 1
LS $=$ 1 then LN $=$ 1

Normally if we made a statement like "if it snows then it is cold" we would expect there to be a reasonable chance of it being true. In such a case LS is $>$ 1 and LN $<$ 1. Thus LS values are normally $1 \leqslant LS \leqslant \infty$ and LN values are normally $0 \leqslant LN \leqslant 1$.

Although LN and LS are related, experts do not always perceive this as true. Often an expert will declare "The presence of E enhances the odds on H, but the absence of E has no effect" ie LS $>$ 1, LN $=$ 1 which is inconsistent. PROSPECTOR is designed to handle this inconsistency.

LS therefore tells us how to alter the prior odds of H if E is true. LN tells us how to alter the prior odds of H if E is untrue. One or other is used depending upon whether E is true or untrue.

5.3.3.2   Uncertain Evidence

But what if E or ~E are not known with certainty? In a perfect world this would be dealt with by interpolation. If we know that E is true with evidence E', eg $P(E\,|\,E')$, then

$$P(H\,|\,E') = P(E\,|\,E').P(H\,|\,E) + (1–P(E\,|\,E').(P(H\,|\,{\sim}E)$$

One problem with this approach is that when the network is set up, all nodes are given prior odds. Since LN/LS relate the prior odds across the network an expert would have great difficulty in setting up a completely consistent network. Experts usually give the prior odds of nodes and the LN, LS values in a subjective (not mathematical) manner. Thus the network will not usually be mathematically consistent. Let E' be the evidence that causes the user to suspect the presence of E. This will alter

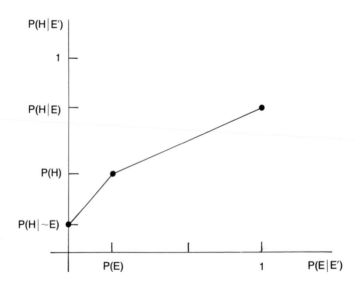

Figure 5.8   Dealing with Uncertain Evidence
(from Reboh R, *Knowledge Engineering Techniques and Tools in the PROSPECTOR Environment*, Technical Note No. 243, June 1981, SRI International, Menlo Park, California, p 18)

the probability of H to $P(H|E')$ which will be between $P(H|\sim E)$ and $P(H|E)$. If $P(E|E')$ has the value 0 then $P(H|E')$ should be $P(H|\sim E)$. When $P(E|E')$ has the value 1, $P(H|E')$ should have the value $P(H|E)$. If however we know nothing about E (ie $P(E|E') = P(E)$) then the prior odds on H should not change. Thus $P(H|E') = P(H)$. These three points give us the relationship between $P(H|E')$ and $P(E|E')$ as shown in Figure 5.8.

This technique overcomes the problem of inconsistent LN, LS and prior odds assigned to the network by the expert. It yields the relationship.

$$P(H|E') = P(H|\sim E) + \frac{(P(H) - P(H|\sim E))}{P(E)} \cdot P(E|E')$$

$$\text{for } 0 \leq P(E|E') \leq P(E)$$

$$\text{and } P(H|E') = P(H) + \frac{(P(H|E) - P(H))}{1 - P(E)} \cdot (P(E|E') - P(E))$$

$$\text{for } P(E) \leq P(E|E') \leq 1$$

It eliminates the propagation of erroneous probabilities through the network due to inconsistent expert values.

The same technique is used to force agreement with user input probability values and the prior odds allocated to the answer-seeking node by the expert. A user is required to give a certainty factor $C(E|E')$ between -5 (negation) and $+5$ (true). The principle used is to define a $C(E|E')$ of 0 as having no effect on the prior probability, a $C(E|E') = 5$ forcing the probability to be 1, and a $C(E|E') = -5$ forcing it to be zero.

This yields a similar piecewise graph (Figure 5.9) between $C(E|E')$ and the probability $P(E)$,

$$\text{giving } P(E|E') = P(E) + \frac{C(E|E')}{5} \cdot (1 - P(E)) \qquad \text{for } C(E|E') > 0$$

$$\text{and } \quad P(E|E') = P(E) + \frac{C(E|E')}{5} \cdot P(E) \qquad \text{for } C(E|E') \leq 0$$

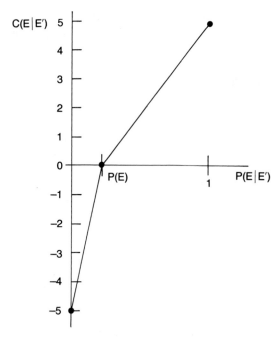

Figure 5.9   Relationship between Certainty and Probability
(from Reboh R, *Knowledge Engineering Techniques and Tools in the PROSPECTOR Environment*, Technical Note No. 243, June 1981, SRI International, Menlo Park, California, p 20)

Thus if the user replied 2 for the certainty of particular evidence E with a prior probability of $P(E) = .2$, then the revised prior probability would be $.2 + (2/5)(.8) = .52$.

5.3.3.3 Logical Relations

The three logical relations used are AND,OR and NOT. When several assertions must all be true for a hypothesis to be true, the truth of the hypothesis is the conjunction of its assertions (AND). When only one assertion of a set need be true then the truth of the hypothesis is the disjunction of the assertions (OR). The third logical operator – negation – merely switches the truth value of the hypothesis. Assertions are therefore combined using AND, OR and NOT.

In general the assertions will not be true or false but rather will have compiled probabilities. In this case Fuzzy Set theory is used. For AND, the minimum probability is taken. For OR the maximum probability is taken, and NOT simply negates the probability.

5.3.3.4   Contextual Relations

These relationships are provided in order to cope with the situation where assertions cannot be considered as being in an arbitrary order. In reality certain evidence must be available before other evidence is sought. In PROSPECTOR models these relations are shown by dashed arrows. The target space must be determined before the space at the head of the arrow is examined. An example is given in Figure 5.5 where the presence of "granitic intrusives in the region" must be determined before the "favourable regional environment".

5.4   CONCLUSIONS

The MYCIN and PROSPECTOR systems discussed in this chapter extend the range of processing tasks capable of being undertaken by computer by enabling a program to cope with various types of uncertainty. Such uncertainty may rest both with the knowledge underlying problem-solving and with the evidence available to the user upon which a conclusion is to be reached.

With regard to domain specific knowledge, the production rule method of representation places no restrictions (in itself) upon the content of the rules. This content can either be knowledge with some theoretical base or empirical knowledge such as "rules of thumb". Hence, it is not necessary for there to be some complete and uniform theoretical description of the area for successful problem-solving to take place. Both types of knowledge may be effectively processed within the same control structure. The production rule form of representation is thus ideal for a subject area in which there is significant empirical knowledge which has perhaps yet to be codified into a principled, formal structure. This is certainly the case with the area of diagnosis and treatment of infections undertaken by MYCIN or in the use of empirically derived geological models as in PROSPECTOR.

In addition to the possibility of integrating different types of knowledge, a "weak" mixture of facts can be processed through the addition of a numeric component expressing the degree of relationship which is believed to exist between them (the necessity and sufficiency factors of

PROSPECTOR and the certainty factor of MYCIN). The second source of uncertainty processed by MYCIN and PROSPECTOR is that of the reliability with which the user believes he has perceived the evidence. The user is required to declare his estimate of this source of uncertainty during the input of evidence. This is then taken into consideration, along with the uncertainty of relationships between evidence, in computing the value of a conclusion.

The production system architecture and probabilistic weighting system adopted in MYCIN and PROSPECTOR have proved remarkably successful for use in diagnostic problem-solving within subject areas in which empirical knowledge predominates. However, there are a number of weaknesses.

Firstly, apart from the context tree in MYCIN and the semantic network in PROSPECTOR, any causal or taxonomic structure within the knowledge encoded in the production rules is not explicitly represented and thus is neither visible to the user nor directly available for processing. The result is that the implications of such knowledge are often opaque to users, leading to difficulties both for understanding conclusions and for debugging or developing a knowledge base. As a result, such systems require an additional "explanation facility" to enable the user to gain knowledge of implications and structure, which with some other form of representation he might have gained directly from the knowledge itself. In addition, the system cannot take advantage of the "expectations" provided by structural knowledge of the results of the current course of reasoning. The system may on occasions continue to pursue some goal which explicit knowledge of the causal relations between items of evidence, for example, would have already indicated as unproductive.

A second problem is that while the simple deductive reasoning process used in MYCIN and PROSPECTOR is intended to be understandable to a user, it is not intended to model the reasoning processes actually adopted by human experts. This has a number of implications. The most serious is to do with questioning. It is well known that in any complex problem-solving, a user's answer to a question will vary with the perceived context of the question. With a conventional rule-based system, there is no explicit indication of reasoning strategy, and thus the context may well be opaque to all but the designer. This problem is likely to be compounded by the mixture of different classes of knowledge being used in the same deduction, so inhibiting the use of structural knowledge to give a rationale for reasoning.

The result is that the MYCIN- and PROSPECTOR-like approaches are most effective for diagnosis within limited and well defined problem areas and where the user already has some reasonable idea of the solution. They are less effective where the solutions are very complex (eg where there are multiple diseases which perhaps share symptoms) or where the user is working with comparative ignorance of the possible solutions.

6 Associative and Causal Approaches to Diagnosis – INTERNIST and CASNET

6.1 INTRODUCTION

The INTERNIST and CASNET projects commenced at about the same time as the systems discussed in Chapter 5. However, they sought to model different aspects of diagnostic reasoning, in some measure addressing the two major criticisms of MYCIN and PROSPECTOR raised in section 5.4 that:

i) there was no attempt to model the reasoning strategies actually used by experts;

ii) there was no attempt to exploit knowledge of causal relations (where they existed).

Attention to diagnostic strategy and causal representation should make expert systems both more understandable and more powerful. Much effort, for example, was invested in the design of explanation facilities for MYCIN and PROSPECTOR to enable them to give a *post hoc* account of their reasoning by exploiting the simple deductive control structure of such systems, either displaying the conclusions resulting from any program state (a Why question) or the conditions necessary for some state to be attained (a How question). However, the lack of explicit structure in both the knowledge base and control processes made it difficult for a user to understand why a particular deduction had been made at a particular point in the diagnosis. Indeed, in TEIRESIAS and GUIDON additional meta-rules were provided for this purpose. Aspects of INTERNIST and CASNET remedy this difficulty, and in doing so enhance diagnostic power.

The INTERNIST project first focused upon automating the actual decision-making techniques used by human clinicians, although a later development within the project also incorporated a significant degree of causal reasoning within the diagnostic logic. The CASNET project set out to develop a diagnostic system based directly on the causal model of a disease. The advantages of this approach include the possibility of identifying a disease at various stages of development and predicting the effect of treatments over time.

6.2 THE INTERNIST PROJECT

6.2.1 General Approach to Diagnosis

The INTERNIST project is based at the University of Pittsburgh and developed from the collaboration of a computer scientist, Pople, and a specialist in internal medicine, Myers. The prototype system – INTERNIST-I – was completed in 1974 and has since undergone regular clinical evaluation and development. In response to difficulties uncovered during such trials, an improved system – INTERNIST-II (also known as CADUCEUS) – is at present under development which incorporates a number of advanced features. These include, for example, a system for reasoning about anatomical structures, and a system for permitting knowledge of the prior treatment of a disease to be taken into consideration during diagnosis. However, this chapter will focus on INTERNIST-I alone.

One notable feature of the INTERNIST systems is that they explicitly seek to model human diagnostic thinking. This is characterised by a two-stage process by which specific disease "manifestations" (eg jaundice, vomiting, or enlarged liver) are linked to specific diseases. The two stages are:

i)   the framing of a diagnostic problem which involves a choice between a set of mutually exclusive disease hypotheses (this is known generally in the clinical literature as a "differential diagnostic model");

ii)   the application of some strategy (which may differ with the characteristics of the model) for resolving the diagnostic problem by identifying a disease from the set which best accounts for the manifestations.

For example, a pain in the chest could be a manifestation of two mutually exclusive "diseases" – angina or indigestion. This is the "differential diagnostic model". The least expensive strategy for resolving this problem might involve the administering of antacid tablets.

At present, INTERNIST is only concerned with diagnosis and does not extend to recommending treatments. Other diagnostic systems primarily addressed the second task of resolving a differential diagnosis, rather than the first task of framing the diagnostic model. MYCIN starts, for example, with an assumption that the disease is bacteriological in origin. However the major problems experienced by clinicians are concerned with the setting up of differential diagnoses. Once this has been achieved, the structure of the diagnostic problem should in itself significantly constrain how evidence is sought and combined.

Observation of expert clinicians at work has shown that diagnostic sessions first involve the setting up of one or more diagnostic tasks. These tasks are then used to guide further data gathering and to establish the final range of alternative diseases considered. Moreover, it was found that the major advantage of "expertise" was that of enabling the clinician to formulate a pertinent set of tasks, not to discriminate between diseases identified within tasks.

A second important finding was that clinical experts formulated differential diagnostic tasks early in a diagnostic session, even though these early tasks were not likely to be correct given an absence of information. However, this lack of accuracy, and hence the high probability that the task would have to be reformulated at a later stage, was outweighed by the advantage of having a clear focus for reasoning. Such a focus provided a context for processing, guided the formulation of hypotheses and the collection of data, and determined the strategy to be used to decide between competing diseases.

Following the above findings, INTERNIST-I initially identifies a set of diseases which account for some or all of the patient's manifestations. Having identified this set of diseases the system attempts to find a single disease from the set which best explains the manifestations. Then follows a process of finding a set of diseases to account for any remaining manifestations, and so on until no symptoms remain to be explained.

6.2.2 Knowledge Representation in INTERNIST-I

INTERNIST-I represents diseases as a hierarchically organised "disease tree". Diseases are linked by the relation "form-of" and are organised into an initial classification tree based on organs (eg liver disease, lung disease) as in Figure 6.1.

Individual disease nodes are classified into those which are non-terminal, which define "disease areas" and those which are terminal, which define "disease entities" (the word 'terminal' being used in a computer science sense rather than a medical sense!). In Figure 6.1, "Hepato-cellular disease" is a disease area and "Acute viral hepatitis" is a disease entity. At present there are over 500 disease entities encoded in the system.

All diseases coded within the tree are actively related to their manifestations via two additional relations, the strength of each relation being represented as a number which may loosely be interpreted as a probability. The first relation is termed "EVOKES". This links a manifestation to the diseases in which it is known to occur (the "evokes-list"), the strength

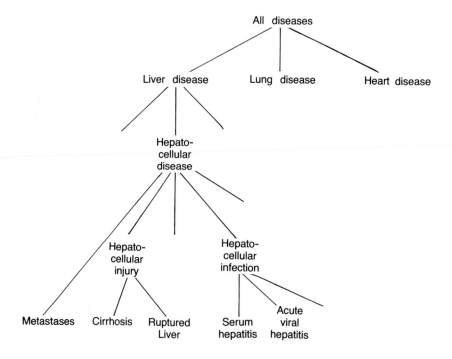

Figure 6.1   A Portion of the INTERNIST-I Disease Tree

of each association represented by a number between 0 and 5, known as the "evoking-strength" of the disease. 0 indicates that no conclusion can be drawn concerning "evoking strength" and 5 indicates that the manifestation necessarily implies the disease. There are at present over 3,500 manifestations recorded in the system.

The inverse of the EVOKES relation is also represented in the system by means of a "MANIFESTS" relation. This points from a disease to a list of its manifestations, the strength of each relation being recorded as an estimate of the frequency with which the manifestation is known to occur with the disease. This estimate is given on a scale of 1 to 5. In addition to the two primary relations (EVOKES, MANIFESTS), a number of other relations are defined on the set of disease entities. These include causal and temporal associations, and are used to aid processing (particularly questioning).

Finally, each manifestation has associated with it two values – TYPE and IMPORT. The TYPE relation records a measure of how expensive it is to test for a manifestation, both in terms of the risk to the patient and financial cost. IMPORT relates a manifestation to a disease and records how important the observation of the manifestation is in order to make a given diagnosis of that disease. The main use of both these relations is for directing processing. The TYPE relation helps in the selection of questions, the least expensive question being addressed first; the IMPORT relation helps establish the priority with which manifestations must be explained. The disease tree and associated relations are kept separate from the knowledge concerning individual consultations, which forms the dynamic part of the program (rather like the context tree in MYCIN).

The above relations are illustrated in Figure 6.2. The figure is intended to aid comprehension rather than give a precise medical description.

The EVOKES relations are labelled with an E followed by the evoking strength in parentheses. Manifestations are denoted by M along with their strength of estimated frequency. The TYPE values are attached to each node, and the IMPORT relations are not shown in the interests of clarity. Note for example that the E strength for enlarged palpable liver is much greater for Cirrhosis than for Metastases. Pyrexia (high temperature) is a key manifestation of Acute Hepatitis (viral or serum). Folate deficiency has a higher TYPE value than enlarged liver because the former requires a laboratory test whilst the latter is a simple procedure.

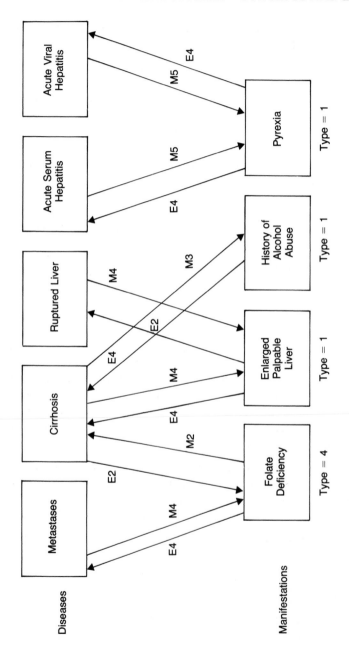

Figure 6.2 Relations in INTERNIST-I

Finally the import of "history of alcohol abuse" would be greater for Cirrhosis than for Metastases.

The diagnostic relations between manifestations and diseases are initially set up to aid efficiency. All appropriate manifestations are first attached to the disease entities at the terminal nodes of the disease tree via both EVOKES and MANIFESTS relations. These are then percolated up the tree. For example, a higher level node will take as its relations the intersection of the sets of all MANIFESTS and EVOKES relations entering from its branches. Moreover, any relation which has been entered in all terminal branches of a node will be stored only at the higher level node. Thus, the usual principle in semantic networks of storing information at the highest level possible is followed. This has two advantages: the usual advantage of economy and a further processing advantage of providing some degree of focus (ie once a manifestation has been found to be present, all nodes below it must be considered in the differential diagnosis). This is illustrated in Figure 6.3 where alphabetic letters indicate manifestations.

6.2.3   The Diagnostic Strategy of INTERNIST-I

During the first phase of a consultation, an initial set of manifestations exhibited by a particular patient are entered into the system, including both positive and pertinent negative findings. Each positive manifestation entered evokes those nodes in the disease tree linked to it, including not only terminal disease entities but also high-level nodes representing a disease category. The latter indicates that the finding can be explained by all subnodes subsumed by the disease category.

The result of entering the initial manifestations is the creation of a "disease model" for each of the disease nodes which has been evoked. These "models" are later used as disease hypotheses for constructing a differential diagnostic task which can be passed forward for testing.

A disease model is created by adding to the evoked disease node four lists of information:

— a list of observed manifestations which are not related to the disease in the network;

— a list of observed manifestations which are related to the disease in the network;

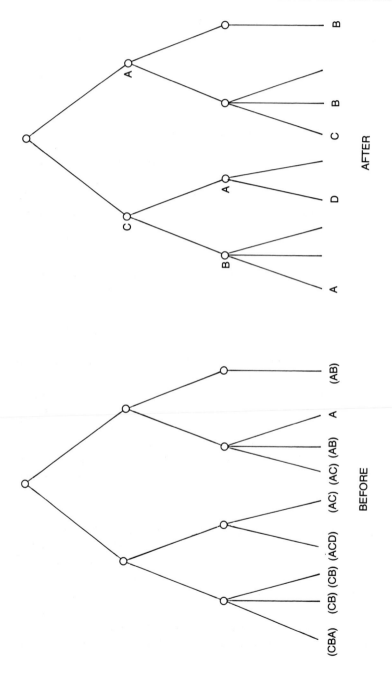

Figure 6.3　The Attachment of "Manifestations" to the Disease Tree

— a list of manifestations which should have been observed if the diagnosis of this disease is correct, but which have not been recorded;

— a list of manifestations attached to the disease which ought to be there but have not been observed in the patient.

Following the construction of these "models", the system begins by formulating its first differential diagnosis. This is done by scoring each disease model, giving a positive point for each manifestation which it explains and a negative point for each not explained. IMPORT provides a further weighting and a bonus point is given if a disease is causally related to some other disease already confirmed. A diagnostic task is then set up from the most highly rated models which provide equally valid explanations for the patient's manifestations. These models, taken together, explain no more of the observed findings than are explained by one or other separately. The set of alternative high-ranking models now become the focus of attention for the second problem-solving stage concerning resolution. Further questions are now asked of the clinician to achieve this.

The process of resolution will depend upon the number of alternative diseases in the set. If there are more than four candidate diseases, then an elimination (RULEOUT) strategy is adopted by which questions are asked which strongly indicate a disease (ie using the IMPORT link). If the relevant manifestation is not present, then the disease is ruled out. If there are between two and four candidates, then a DISCRIMINATE strategy is adopted. Here questions concerning manifestations which strongly indicate one disease but which weakly indicate another one are asked. If there is only one candidate then questions that have a good chance of confirming the disease are asked. Finally, in the case in which there is not enough information to confirm one specific disease, a more general diagnosis is given in terms of classes of diseases.

Once new information has been obtained via one of the questioning procedures listed above, all evoked disease models (whether in or out of the current diagnostic task) are re-evaluated and a new differential diagnosis is constructed. This revised task may vary considerably from its predecessor depending on which diseases have emerged as those most highly rated, thus shifting the attention of the system. This process will continue through successive iterations, until some disease has been confirmed. At this point, all of its manifestations are marked as "accounted for" and bonus points are awarded to all evoked disease causally related to it. The processing then continues in an attempt to explain any remaining manifestations until all diagnostic problems in the case have been solved. Given this procedure, INTERNIST-I may well uncover a number of diseases present in the patient. This is an advance on more conventional medical diagnostic systems which make the simplifying assumption that only one disease is present.

6.2.4 INTERNIST-I Conclusions

A significant feature of INTERNIST-I is that it follows the strategy of constructing and then resolving differential diagnoses used by human clinicians. The model of diagnosis used by the system thus involves the two-stage procedure of first setting up disease hypotheses by the entering of patient data (a bottom-up process) and then evaluating them using the additional manifestations which they imply should be present (a top-down process).

INTERNIST-I is regularly used on an experimental basis within the laboratory. It has proved to be capable of expert performance in complex cases involving multiple diseases, and it is expected that a development of the system will eventually be adopted in routine clinical use. In one trial involving a random selection of 19 cases and 45 anatomically verified diseases (which fell within the scope of INTERNIST's database), INTERNIST-I correctly diagnosed 25 against 28 diagnosed by hospital clinicians.

During clinical trials two practical problems have emerged, one of which has been largely remedied in INTERNIST-II (CADUCEUS) and the other being a current topic of investigation. The first problem is that INTERNIST-I has the tendency of initially focusing on totally inappropriate disease models. This was found by clinicians to be annoying and to lead to understanding difficulties. The source of the problem proved to be the serial nature of INTERNIST-I's processing, which was remedied in INTERNIST-II by introducing a measure of parallelism in the analysis of differential diagnoses.

INTERNIST-II uses the same "disease tree" as INTERNIST-I but augments it with significant additional causal knowledge and a set of so-called "CONSTRICTOR" relations. These act as manifestations which define a general class of disease (represented as a sub-tree of the disease tree). Using these relations, INTERNIST-II successively partitions the disease tree until only terminal nodes (ie disease entities) remain.

The second problem concerns the explanation of a diagnosis. The relations between manifestations and diseases used in INTERNIST-I are largely associational and thus do not attempt to model any disease processes. Diseases are considered as static categories and diagnosis is defined as the assignment of a patient to one or more categories. While this may provide for effective identification of illness, it makes it difficult to provide a convincing explanation facility because of the lack of an explicit, detailed account of the motivation behind questions. This was a problem addressed early in the history of knowledge-based computer diagnosis by the CASNET system to be discussed next. However, it is also being addressed by the INTERNIST group within the INTERNIST-II project, exploiting the enhanced knowledge of causal relations in the system.

6.3 CASNET

6.3.1 Viewing a Disease as a Process

The semantic network form of representation has been used widely for the modelling of causal knowledge, the nodes representing system states and the arcs causal relations. It was therefore natural that semantic networks should be used as the basic representational format for the CASNET (Causal ASsociational NETwork) system developed by Kulikowski and Weiss at Rutgers University in the early and middle 1970s. The objective of the project was to develop and explore computer-based diagnostic strategies founded on physiological and functional models of a disease.

CASNET views disease as a dynamic process involving transformations between pathophysiological states. Diagnosis thus is defined as the identification of a relationship between a pattern of causal pathways observed in the patient with a disease category.

The process description of disease used by CASNET has a number of advantages. First, the causal model can be used to predict the likely path of a disease both if treated and untreated. This is of use in making decisions concerning treatments, in particular for deciding when treatment should be applied. Secondly, the system can be used to model the patient's progress over time.

The domain used for the development of CASNET was that of glaucoma (although the CASNET approach is equally applicable to other diseases about which sufficient is known to give a full causal description). Glaucoma is a disease arising from raised pressure within the eye, and if not treated can cause blindness. It is a particularly suitable domain for the exploration of a causal diagnostic model. The effects of glaucoma are restricted to the eye, which has very few structures and thus can be fairly completely described. Moreover, the processes of glaucoma and the treatment of the disease are fairly well understood and the effects can be relatively accurately measured.

6.3.2 Representation of Knowledge in CASNET

The basic CASNET clinical model consists of four "planes of knowledge", three of which describe the disease itself – Figure 6.4 – and one of which describes treatment plans.

At the centre of the disease model is a description of "pathophysiological states". The description is cast in the form of a semantic network, the nodes representing physiological states (which form the disease hypotheses of the system) and the arcs representing causal connections between disease states. An example of a disease state might be "cupping of the optic disc" and "elevated intraocular pressure". A complete pathway from a start state to a terminal state usually represents a complete disease process, and progression along a pathway represents increasing seriousness of the disease.

Associated with each causal relationship is a confidence factor. This is given as a number between 1 and 5, where 1 corresponds to "rarely causes" and 5 corresponds to "(almost) always causes".

The level below the "plane of pathophysiological states" is the "plane of observations". Here the nodes represent the symptoms and manifestations which may possibly be associated with the various stages of the disease, and each of them is related to some observational constraints such as the "cost" of making an observation (in terms of danger or financial cost) or the pre-conditions of collecting the evidence (eg the cap-to-disc ratio at the optic nerve head can be determined only if an ophthalmoscopic examination is performed). Each of the "observations" is linked to disease states, the relationship between observations and

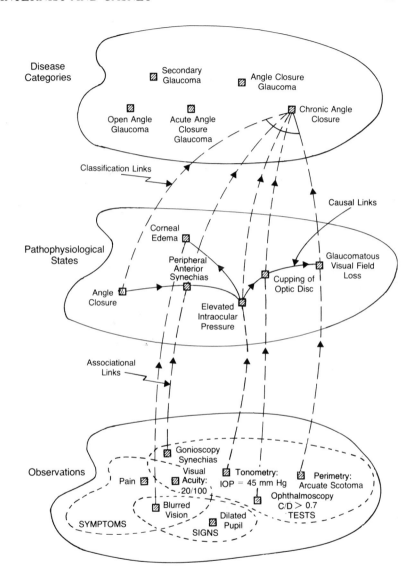

Figure 6.4 Three-Level Description of a Disease Process
(from Weiss S M, Kulikowski C A, Amaral S and Safir A, 1978, A
model-based method for computer-aided medical decision-making,
Artificial Intelligence, 11, North-Holland Publishing Co, p 148 and p 166)

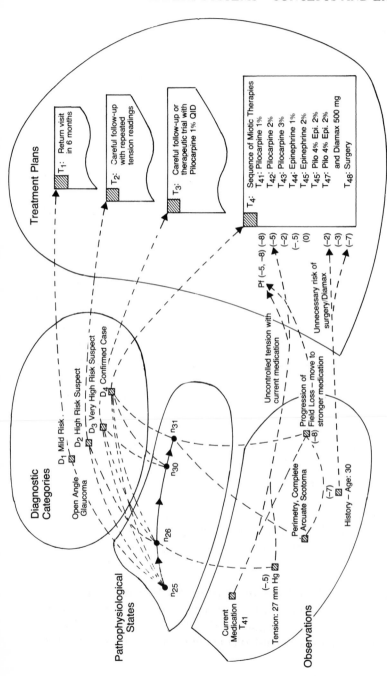

Figure 6.5   The CASNET Model for Disease Processes and Treatment

(from Weiss S M, Kulikowski C A, Amaral S and Safir A, 1978, A model-based method for computer-aided medical decision-making, *Artificial Intelligence*, 11, North-Holland Publishing Co, p 148 and p 166)

diseases often being "many-to-many" ie each state may have many "observations" related to it and each observation may indicate more than one disease state. Finally, the links are also weighted from 1 to 5, reflecting the degree to which a particular sign, symptom or test supports an associated state.

The plane above the "plane of pathophysiological states" contains a higher-level classification of diseases. These classifications – eg acute angle closure glaucoma – are linked to a pattern of pathophysiological states, which are either confirmed or denied as a consultation progresses. Finally, the "disease states", and indirectly the "pathophysiological states", are linked to a set of "treatment plans". These are linked among themselves by constraints of interaction, time dependence, toxicity, etc. Figure 6.5 shows all four levels.

6.3.3 The Diagnostic Process in CASNET

The general diagnostic strategy employed by CASNET is that of finding one or more causal pathways between pathophysiological states. To this end, a diagnostic session begins with the clinicians being questioned by the system concerning the patient's symptoms. As these are entered they set the value of the states to "confirmed", "denied" or "unknown". These values are then combined with the confidence factors on the causal arcs and the weightings associated with some observational constraints to compute a confidence factor for each pathophysiological state. A state is declared as "confirmed" if its value passes some pre-determined threshold and denied if it is below a second threshold. Moreover, the order in which questions are asked will depend upon the value indicating the cost of collecting evidence.

Once all "observations" have been entered, an interpretation of the disease process is first made with reference to the plane of pathophysiological states. Given the representation of a disease as a causal network, the most likely cause of the patient's problem is defined as the "start state" in the network from which pathways are generated that traverse the greatest number of confirmed nodes (and contain no denied nodes). If more than one such start state is found, then a likelihood measure is computed for the states and the one with the greatest weight is selected. If any one start state is unable to generate pathways which traverse all confirmed states, then additional paths are sought through the remaining confirmed states. For example, in Figure 6.4 "angle closure" is a start state which leads via the pathway of "elevated intraocular pressure" and "peripheral anterior synechias" to "cupping of the optic disc" and finally to "glaucomatous visual field loss". However, note that the same start state may also lead to "corneal edema".

Having identified one or more causal pathways which represent the current status of the patient, the "plane of disease categories" and the treatment plans are used to select a therapy. Classes of disease are described in a set of "identification tables", which summarise the pathways present in the "plane of pathophysiological states" as a set of rules and are initially selected by a pointer from the start state of a pathway. Of course, several different start states may point to the same table because several causal mechanisms may be included in the same diagnostic category. For an individual patient, the most likely start states are used to identify the appropriate tables. The rules in each of the tables will then be applied to link the confirmed set of disease states to a disease classification, the classification being selected within each table which accounts for the deepest confirmed state. In Figure 6.4, the disease pathways point to category "chronic angle closure". Finally, at the end of the classification process, appropriate treatments may be read off for each confirmed disease category, care being taken to identify cases when some treatment is subsumed by another.

6.3.4 CASNET Conclusions

The current CASNET system has more than "100 states, 400 tests, 75 classification tables and 200 diagnostic and treatment statements". The consultation program is written in FORTRAN in the interest of speed, while the modification of the glaucoma model is carried out in interaction with a SNOBOL program.

The diagnostic strategy used in CASNET may be summarised in terms of a series of transformations: test results and observations are related to individual pathophysiological states as they are received; the states so confirmed or denied are organised into pathways inferred from the state network; these pathways are related to classification tables containing diagnostic categories; disease categories are used as the basis for selecting treatments. The diagnostic approach adopted by CASNET is thus strictly bottom-up, working from observations to treatments.

The CASNET system has been systematically evaluated and achieves expert performance in the long-term diagnosis and treatment of many types of glaucoma. For example, a 95% acceptance rate for clinical proficiency is quoted for a trial in which ophthalmologists were encouraged to test the system with difficult cases at a clinical meeting (45 cases) with 77% of cases rated as being diagnosed at "expert" or "very competent" levels.

Finally, it should be noted that the "model-based" approach to diagnosis used by CASNET has one significant advantage over other diagnostic methods. The explicit representation of disease processes within the "plane of pathophysiological states" allows the system to be used to follow the patient's progress over time. Hence, the disease model may be used to record the patient's response to treatment, evaluate possible treatments and as a method of exploring and evaluating possible alternative causes of a disease. Moreover, the causal pathways terminating at a confirmed node provide a comprehensible explanation of the diagnosis to that point, while unconfirmed nodes past that point give a measure of expectation concerning the future course of the disease.

7 Reducing Large Search Spaces Through Factoring – Heuristic DENDRAL and Meta-DENDRAL

7.1 PROCESSING LARGE SEARCH SPACES

It may be recalled that in Chapter 3 we introduced the Artificial Intelligence idea of "state-space search". According to this paradigm, problem-solving is seen as involving a search through a network of nodes, each representing a possible problem state. Moreover, it was also pointed out that with any real-world domain the state-space will tend to be very large, so making it undesirable (or even impossible) to obtain solutions through an exhaustive search of the space. A major focus of research has been the development of techniques for "controlling" state-space search so as to enable systems to cope with large state-spaces. Effective control methods tend to be specific to the type of relationships that exist between the states of the problem and, in particular, to the relative independence of the states.

One well-known technique for dealing with large search spaces is called "generate-and-test". Starting at some initial state, a "generator" is used to produce a set of "offspring" states. Then a series of validity tests are applied to the set of offspring states to reduce it to a more manageable size. These tests are usually in the form of constraints. It is often possible to build some of these constraints into the generator, thereby reducing the number of offspring states to be tested. The "generate-and-test" approach will only work if, when a state is declared invalid, it follows that all offspring states will also be invalid. Thus effective pruning at an early stage will dramatically reduce the number of candidate states.

For example, if one considers the first move in a game of chess, one could generate all possible moves of every piece. A test could be made to invalidate all moves which crossed a square already occupied by a "home" piece (except for the knight). Another test after generation could be concerned with checking whether the move has opened up the possibility of deploying, say a bishop on the next move. However it would be more effective to incorporate the first test into the generation phase thereby reducing the number of tests to be made.

The "generate-and-test" method of controlling the exploration of a search space was adopted for the DENDRAL programs. Heuristic DENDRAL and Meta-DENDRAL were, effectively, the first knowledge-based expert systems. The DENDRAL systems were developed by a large research group at Stanford University and were concerned with various aspects of the elucidation of the structure of compounds in organic chemistry. The project was begun in 1965 with the explicit objective of providing computer support for professional chemists who were not necessarily experts in particular analytical techniques. Moreover, such was its success that it inspired the development of the whole expert systems area of Artificial Intelligence.

7.2　THE APPLICATION TASK

The determination of the structure of chemical molecules is of fundamental interest in many areas of biology and medicine. The simplest method of doing this is to directly examine the structure using X-ray crystallography. However, this is not always possible, in which case the chemist has to resort to other methods, including infra-red analysis, ultraviolet analysis, "wet chemistry" and mass spectrometry. In each case, the chemist will undertake his structural analysis in a number of stages:

— having obtained his sample, he will apply tests of the type mentioned above;

— this data will be interpreted to provide a number of structural hypotheses concerning possible functional groups or more complex molecular fragments which could make up the molecule under investigation;

— the fragments will be assembled into complete structures to provide a set of candidate structures for the unknown molecule;

— the candidates are examined and experiments designed to differentiate between them;

— the experiments are executed, probably involving the collection of additional data, providing more structural information to further reduce the set of candidate structures;

— eventually enough information will be available to constrain the set of candidates to enable the correct structure to be determined.

When there are only a small number of candidate structures, it is possible to conduct the process manually. However when there are a large number, the procedure can be aided to a significant degree by computer assistance. The DENDRAL project aimed to design such tools. The first program was Heuristic DENDRAL (to be referred to simply as DENDRAL). This is the basic expert system and is designed to help chemists to determine the structure of some unknown compound, with special reference to the use of data from a mass spectrometer.

A mass spectrometer is a device which bombards the sample of a chemical compound with electrons, causing the "fragmentation" and rearrangement of the molecules. The resulting charged fragments are then separated out by their mass, the results being presented as a histogram of the number of fragments at a particular mass. Figure 7.1 is just such a histogram which is more correctly called a mass spectrum.

One advantage of mass spectrometry is that it only requires very small samples, using only micrograms of the compound. However, there can be serious interpretation problems. While the mass spectrum for each molecule is nearly unique, it is difficult to infer the molecular structure from the 100 to 300 data points in it. Moreover, the data may also be very redundant because molecules fragment along different pathways.

The knowledge used for interpreting mass spectra in Heuristic DENDRAL was collected from experts. However, there were difficulties. The process was very time consuming; much of the experts' knowledge of mass spectrometry being tacit and thus not easily expressed. This problem is very clearly illustrated in the following passage which records the opening discussion of a knowledge elicitation session (after Buchanan). It also gives a feel for the type of knowledge manipulated by DENDRAL. "C" is the expert chemist and "KE", the knowledge engineer, seeking to elicit information and to cast it into a form which can be used by DENDRAL.

C: Since El Supremo and the rest want us to work on ketones, I guess we should get started.

KE: Why are ketones important?

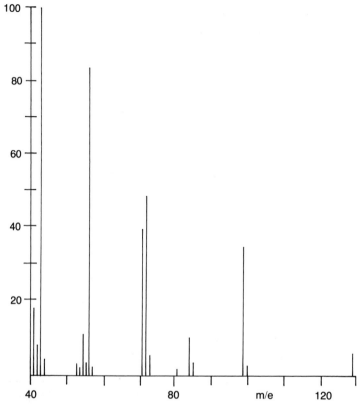

Composition: $C_8H_{16}O$
Molecular Weight (M) = 128

Molecular Structure: $CH_3–CH_2–\overset{\overset{O}{\|}}{C}–CH_2–CH_2–CH_2–CH_2–CH_3$

Computer Representation of the Mass Spectrum:

((41 . 18)(42 . 7)(43 . 100)(44 . 3)
(53 . 3)(54 . 1)(55 . 11)(56 . 3)
(57 . 80)(58 . 2)(70 . 1)(71 . 36)
(72 . 44)(73 . 5)(81 . 1)(85 . 6)
(86 . 2)(99 . 31)(100 . 2)(128 . 5))

Figure 7.1   Mass Spectrum for Compound 3-octanone
(from Buchanan B, Sutherland G and Feigenbaum E A, 1969,
HEURISTIC DENDRAL: a program for generating explanatory
hypotheses in organic chemistry, in B Meltzer and D Michie (eds),
Machine Intelligence, 4, Edinburgh University Press, p 210)

C: Besides being very common in organic chemistry we also know something of their mass spectrometry because they've been studied a lot.

KE: What subgraph exactly will cause a molecule to be classed as a ketone?

C: The keto, or carbonyl, radical. That is $-C=O$ (noticing KE's puzzled look).

KE: Then all of these are ketones?
$$CH_3-CH_2-C=O-R$$
$$CH_3-C=O-R$$
$$H-C=O-R$$

C: Wait a minute. The first two are ketones, but the last one is a special case which we should distinguish in the program. It defines the class of aldehydes.

KE: So can we formulate the general rule that a ketone is any molecule containing $C-C=O-C$?

C: That's it.

KE: Now what mass spectrometry rules do you have for ketones?

C: Three processes will dominate: alpha-cleavage, elimination of carbon monoxide from the alpha-cleavage fragments, and the McLafferty re-arrangements.

KE: OK. I wrote those down – now tell me exactly what each one means. Start with alpha-cleavage – do you mean the bond next to the heteroatom?

C: (Digression on notation – often alpha-cleavage would mean this bond, but not for mass spectrometry) . . . Here alpha-cleavage is cleavage of the $C-C=O$ bond, ie cleavage next to the carbonyl radical – on both sides don't forget.

KE: All right. That's an easy rule to put in. Shall we say the peaks are always high?

C: That will do as a start. We don't really pay much attention to intensities just as long as the peaks show up.

(Reasons why exact intensities cannot be computed are explained briefly – KE's interpretation is that chemists just don't know enough about them.)

In response to the above elicitation problems, a second program was developed – Meta-DENDRAL – to aid the process of generating effective sets of rules to express constraints. Meta-DENDRAL is discussed in section 7.4.

7.3 HEURISTIC DENDRAL

7.3.1 The DENDRAL Planning Program

The basic control process employed by DENDRAL is a "generate-and-test" sequence, as was described in section 7.1. However, in practice it was found an additional "planning" program was required in order to produce constraints to be used by the generator and testing programs. The full cycle is thus one of "Plan – Generate – Test", ie careful planning greatly limits unwanted generation, thus simplifying the testing phase.

In a similar manner to MYCIN, DENDRAL does not pretend that it is simulating the interpretative processes used by chemists. However, it does claim that it complements their methods by undertaking such a careful search through the space of possible molecular structures that the final list of candidate structures will accurately reflect the decisions a chemist would have made (given adequate time).

At the start of an analytic session (the planning phase) using Heuristic DENDRAL the chemist employs the planning program to infer lists of necessary and forbidden substructures from a mass spectrum of the compound to be analysed. These lists – known as GOODLIST and BADLIST respectively – will later help to constrain the structures contributed by the generator, so reducing the number of plausible configurations which need to be evaluated by the testing program.

The relevant mass spectrum (eg the 3-octanone mass spectrum in Figure 7.1) is given to the planner along with a list of the atomic constituents of the molecule. The planner then applies to this raw data a considerable quantity of knowledge concerning mass spectrometry, to infer the probable classification of the substance (eg that it probably contains a ketone group – a GOODLIST fact – but it is definitely not a methyl-ketone – a BADLIST fact). The knowledge is coded as production rules of the form:

IF   *THEN*

Rule 1: There are 2 peaks at mass units x1 and x2   KETONE
     such that
     a) x1 + x2 = M + 28
     b) x1 − 28 is a high peak
     c) x2 − 28 is a high peak
     d) At least one of x1 or x2 is high

Rule 2: a) Ketone conditions are satisfied   METHYL–KETONE–3
     b) 43 is a high peak
     c) 58 is a high peak
     d) M − 43 is a low peak
     e) M − 15 is low or possibly zero

Rule 3: a) Ketone conditions are satisfied   ETHYL–KETONE–3
     b) 57 is a high peak
     c) 72 is a high peak
     d) M − 29 is a high peak
     e) M − 57 is a high peak

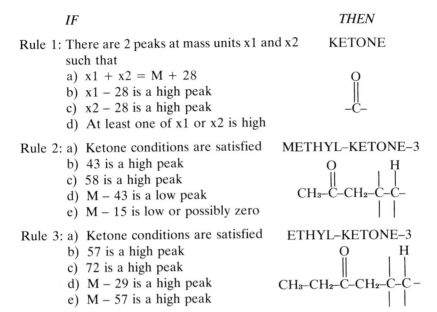

Taking the mass spectrum given in figure 7.1 the planner first applies general rules, such as Rule 1, which tests for ketones. Checking the conditions against the spectrum it is found that:

    a) x1 + x2 = M + 28 = 156 for the following peaks (56 + 100, 57+99, 70+86, 71+85)
    b) x1 − 28 is high for the solution x1 = 71
    c) x2 − 28 is high for the solution x2 = 85
    d) x1 or x2 is high for the solution x1 = 71

and thus the unknown must contain a ketone group.

Given the success of Rule 1, the planner may now forward chain to consider those rules which have the presence of a ketone group as one of their conditions. Rules 2 and 3 are examples of such rules. However, if the reader carries out the comparison with Figure 7.1 it will be found that the conditions of Rule 3 match whilst those of Rule 2 do not. As these are rules at the highest level, the system concludes that the unknown substance contains an "ethyl-ketone-3" group but definitely does not contain a "methyl-ketone-3" group. Ethyl-ketone-3 is thus put on the GOODLIST and methyl-ketone-3 is put on the BADLIST. In certain circumstances it is also possible for the planner to determine the position of a functional group, in which case this additional information is noted for later use by the generator.

Many of the planner's production rules can have a dramatic effect in reducing the possible number of structures which have to be considered. For example, the knowledge that a spectrum contains 8 carbon atoms, 16 hydrogen atoms and 1 oxygen atom reduces the number of topologically possible structures from 698 to 3, sending to the BADLIST all structures except those containing ethyl-ketone-3. However, in general such dramatic reductions are not possible so that the information obtained at the end of the planning phase is confined to a list of principal structures. The GOODLIST and BADLIST results are therefore now passed on to the structure generator for further determination.

7.3.2 DENDRAL Structure Generators

At the centre of DENDRAL is a program which generates the search space of possible chemical structures. The initial generator was one already available at the outset of the project, being designed by Lederberg at Stanford. This program systematically enumerated molecular structures, treating them as planar graphs and generating successively larger structures, until all atoms were included in all possible arrangements. There were, however, problems with this system; principally that it was unconstrained, and thus generated many structures which an expert chemist would readily have eliminated, or would never have considered in the first place. The present version of DENDRAL therefore employs a more sophisticated generator known as CONGEN, which was designed in 1976 and stands for "CONstrained GENerator". This limits the search space to only plausible structures. The constraints are input by the chemist undertaking the analysis and may include such factors as the number of atoms of each type of molecule and hypothesised atomic relationships in the molecule.

CONGEN operates by breaking down the problem into different classes of subproblem. These concern, for example:

1) the problem of omitting hydrogen atoms until the end of the generation process;

2) the separation of parts of the graph containing no cycles from the cyclic parts (and combination in the end);

3) generating cycles containing only unnamed nodes before label-

ling the nodes with names of atoms;

4) the generation of cycles containing only three-connected (or higher) nodes (eg nitrogen or tertiary carbon) before mapping two connected nodes (eg oxygen or tertiary carbon) onto the edges.

At each stage the number of emerging structures may be limited by the allocation of several constraints, and the user may interact with the program to add constraints at will. There are three classes: graph theoretic (symmetric structures are not considered to be unique); syntactic (certain structures will not be plausible because of the valencies of constituent atoms); semantic (including additional information concerning the molecule derived from other tests, etc). Moreover, the chemists may interrupt the program at any point to add information.

Although CONGEN was developed to function as part of Heuristic DENDRAL, it may be used on its own. It thus does not simply provide a one-shot generation of structures to be used by the other DENDRAL programs, but should rather be seen as a set of structure generation facilities. These may either be used under DENDRAL's control, or under the control of the human chemist.

7.3.3 The Testing Program

The testing of generated structures is performed by two programs, MSPRUNE and MSRANK. First, MSPRUNE takes each candidate structure and generates a hypothetical mass spectrum for it. This is achieved using a fairly simple model of a mass spectrometer, which is encoded as a set of production rules concerning the ways molecules fragment under bombardment. These artificially generated mass spectra are then compared with the real mass spectrum of the unknown molecule, and any synthesised structures which deviate significantly are pruned away.

The remaining candidate structures are finally ranked by the program MSRANK. This employs a more subtle set of rules of mass spectrometry to order the structures according to the number of predicted peaks found (or not found) in the original mass spectrum, weighted by the importance of the processes producing the peaks.

Both MSPRUNE and MSRANK represent their knowledge of cleavage and migration within a mass spectrometer as a set of production rules.

An example of a simple rule describing fragmentation is:

IF N–C–C–C THEN N–C*C–C

This asserts that if a molecule with a graph structure N–C–C–C fragments then a bond will break between the first and second carbon atoms to give the two fragments N–C and C–C. These fragments will be recorded as a peak at the point of the mass spectrum corresponding to their molecular weight. Atom migrations are represented using a similar rule format.

7.3.4 Evaluation of Heuristic DENDRAL

Figure 7.2 gives an overview of the Heuristic DENDRAL system, and is presented to help the reader appreciate the relationship between the planning, generation and testing modules.

Heuristic DENDRAL has an important place in the history of expert system research because it demonstrated the possibility of designing a computer-based problem-solver capable of achieving expert performance in a limited area of science. The designers claim that although the system knows less than an expert, the care with which the limited knowledge is applied more than adequately compensates. Hence, Heuristic DENDRAL has been shown to give expert analysis of a number of substances, including oliphatic ketones, amines, ethers, alcohols and estrogenic steroids.

One of the major problems in the design of DENDRAL was the development of an efficient set of rules for constraining molecular structure. As mentioned in section 7.2, expert chemists often had difficulty in framing rules because much of their knowledge was tacit or the compound of interest was outside their area of expertise. The Meta-DENDRAL project was undertaken to remedy these problems.

7.4 META-DENDRAL

7.4.1 Objectives

Two approaches have been adopted in attempting to solve the problem of formulating knowledge of mass spectrometry as production rules. The first was to provide an interactive interface similar to the TEIRESIAS program used for the transfer of expertise to MYCIN and discussed in Chapter 5. The second involved the automatic formulation of general

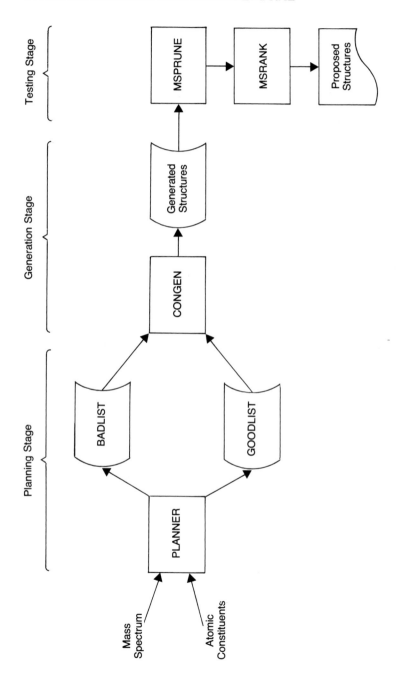

Figure 7.2   An Overview of Heuristic DENDRAL

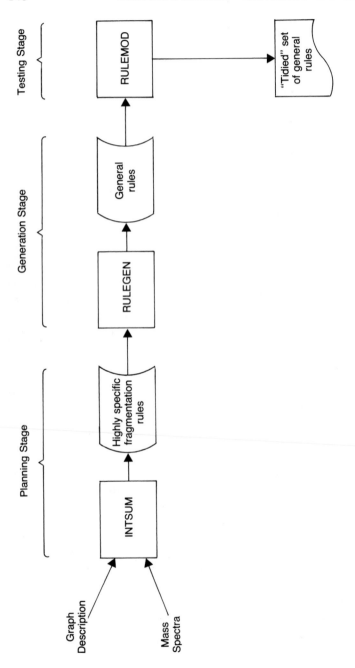

Figure 7.3   An Overview of Meta-DENDRAL

rules from examples. It is this latter approach which has been explored in Meta-DENDRAL, principally with reference to the generation of the rules used in the testing phase of Heuristic DENDRAL to simulate atomic fragmentation and migration, and to predict data points. The system is illustrated in Figure 7.3.

7.4.2 Rule Generation Process

The objective of Meta-DENDRAL is to generate a general set of fragmentation rules for some predetermined class of molecules. This is achieved using a structural description and related mass spectrum for each of the molecules in the class under a "plan-generate-test" control structure. The three programs involved are INTSUM (data INTerpretation and SUMmary) – the planner, RULEGEN – the generator, and RULEMOD – the tester.

The rule generation process begins with what is termed a "training phase". Here the program INTSUM is required to produce a set of highly specific bond cleavage rules for specific families of molecules. These families typically include 6 to 10 related molecules which have been found to follow a similar cleavage pattern. The process is achieved using three types of data:

 i) the graph structure descriptions for the set of molecules;

 ii) a description of the empirically derived mass spectrum for each of the molecules;

 iii) a "semantic theory" of cleavage in a mass spectrometer which is used to constrain the generation process.

The "semantic theory" of bond cleavage used in Meta-DENDRAL is termed a "half-order" theory. This was developed to compare a rather specific set of constraints on rule generation. The "half-order" theory gets its name in contrast to the base-level, or "zero-order" theory which asserts that every subset of bonds within a molecule may break and that all the resulting fragments, plus or minus migrating atoms, will be recorded. However, the actual constraints corresponding to the real behaviour of molecules under bombardment are more complex and require more specific guidelines. These guidelines are therefore termed "half-order" and include such constraints on cleavage as:

—   double bonds and triple bonds do not break;

— two bonds to the same carbon atom cannot break together;

— only fragments larger than two carbon atoms show up in the data;

and on migration as:

— at most two hydrogen atoms can migrate after a fragmentation;

— at most one H_2O unit is lost after any fragmentation.

The task of INTSUM is first to apply the cleavage rules to each molecule in order to explain each peak in its related mass spectrum. To constitute an acceptable explanation for a peak, the fragmentation rules will only include those allowed under the half-order theory described above and must produce fragments which correspond to peaks in the mass spectrum. Once a set of explanations has been provided for each of the peaks in the spectrum, INTSUM summarises the results. This second stage is necessary since any given fragmentation process may account for a number of different peaks.

At the close of the planning phase, INTSUM will have generated a set of highly specific rules which account for a single fragmentation process in a particular molecule. The task of the generator program RULEGEN is to use these highly specific rules as input and to generate from them a more general set using the positive training instances from INTSUM. In broad terms, this is achieved by first identifying notable features of molecular structure around the fragmentation site identified by INTSUM, which are then combined to form a subgraph description of the atomic environment surrounding a broken bond. This subgraph is used as the conditional "IF" part of a candidate rule, the action "THEN" part being the cleavage process proposed by INTSUM.

The generalisation process is accomplished by first developing a tree of fragmentation rules (starting with the totally general rule that fragmentation takes place between two structures) which is progressively refined by adding features until it becomes more constrained. These features include the identity of fragments, the number of non-hydrogen neighbours, the number of hydrogen neighbours and the number of double-bonded neighbours. As features are added the new rule is evaluated for "improvement" using a computed "improvement criterion" concerning the ability of the new rule to predict bond cleavage compared with its parent rule. When it is found that the value of the improvement index begins to decline, no further features are added and the rule is output.

Once a set of candidate rules have been generated by RULEGEN, it is necessary to test their validity. This is primarily because RULEGEN ignores "negative evidence" concerning the incorrect prediction of peaks and is therefore likely to produce some rules which are either incorrect or redundant. This "tidying up" process is achieved by RULEMOD which seeks to remove redundancy in the rule set, merge related rules which are too specific to form a more general rule and eliminate negative evidence by making other rules more specific.

The result of the entire sequence is a set of fragmentation rules for mass spectra which are "specialised enough to be interesting but which are general enough to be efficient and which are non-redundant".

7.4.3 Meta-DENDRAL Conclusions

Meta-DENDRAL has been evaluated using generated learned rules to predict the mass spectra of new molecules. This has been successfully achieved. Not only has the system rediscovered known rules of mass spectrometry for two classes of molecule, but it has also discovered new rules for "three closely related families of structures for which the rules had not been previously reported".

An interesting development of Meta-DENDRAL is its successful application to a difference spectroscopy technique; that of BC-nuclear magnetic resonance spectroscopy. In this context, Meta-DENDRAL generates rules which associate the resonance frequency of a carbon atom in a magnetic field with the local structural environment of the atom.

8 Handling Large Search Spaces Through the Use of Abstraction – R1 and MOLGEN

8.1 LEVELS OF DESCRIPTION IN A SEARCH SPACE

The "generate-and-test" method of reducing a large search space, illustrated in the previous chapter, is most readily applicable when the space factors cleanly into a number of independent sub-spaces. However there are many problem areas which do not factor in this way. The most notable are those involving problems of design and planning where it is often not possible to define in advance the precise goal state to be reached. Although it may be possible to give some general description, this will not be sufficiently constrained to allow for effective pruning of solution paths. The danger is that pruning may cut away part of the search zone which, while initially appearing unpromising, may in fact provide a solution later in processing when more information becomes available. However, once cut away, a section of search space can never be considered again.

An important alternative approach which was initially developed within Artificial Intelligence for planning problems is that of "abstracting" the search space. This may be illustrated using the familiar example concerning the problem of finding the shortest route between two places – for example, from the University of Liverpool to the University of Strathclyde, in Glasgow. One possible approach would be to find a large-scale map (or set of maps) including both cities and to proceed by tracing all possible routes between the two Universities (omitting all circular routes), noting the length of each as it is traced. The shortest could then simply be found by inspection.

The flaw with the above strategy is obvious. There are many hundreds of roads in both Liverpool and Glasgow, all of which will need to be explored along with all the towns that can be connected to both. The task of finding the shortest route by an exhaustive search of all possible roads given in a detailed map will be a massive one. In reality, of course, we would never approach the task in this way. Instead, we would consult a number of maps, each with a scale appropriate to a phase of the journey. The central portion of the journey taking us from Liverpool to Glasgow would be planned using a small-scale map showing only the main roads and motorways, this level of detail being appropriate to the distance being covered. Navigation through the terminal cities, and any towns or cities along the way, would be guided by medium-scale maps showing the main streets, while the route within the immediate area of the Universities would be guided by a detailed street map showing individual buildings.

The principle behind the selection of maps in the above example is that they show just sufficient detail for the travel task in hand. Put in other terms, the "level of abstraction" of each map should be such as to enable each stage of the route finding task to be performed as efficiently as possible without unnecessary search. The hierarchical organisation of the three levels of map enable the solution to be initially sketched out in general terms, resulting in the identification of additional sub-problems which can then be tackled using a more detailed description of the territory. The use of a set of successively more abstract descriptions of the problem space thus has three strengths. It provides a basis for structuring a problem into a set of sub-problems; it provides a search space for each sub-problem which is appropriate to the goals behind that stage of processing; and the contents of the search space at each level provide an appropriate focus for the efficient gathering of evidence at that level. By presenting salient functions for processing at each level, a complete route may be planned at that level without the need to cope with local details. Working at normal levels of abstraction thus enables us to home in on a solution. This avoids the problem of finding a route which fails only after one has explored it in considerable depth, necessitating substantial back-tracking before an effective route is found. The "generate-and-test" procedure described in the previous chapter also has this objective, although in the present example there is not likely to be sufficient information to make an effective test until the end of a path has been reached, by which time it is too late to achieve any savings.

Several expert systems have employed abstraction as a method of reducing the very large search space of the problem domain. There are, however, differences in the criteria used for decomposition. To illustrate two different uses of the technique, we will discuss in this chapter the R1 system (developed by McDermott at Carnegie-Mellon University for configuring Digital Equipment Corporation VAX computers) and the MOLGEN planner (developed by Stefik at Stanford University for the design of genetics experiments). The R1 program uses a simple form of abstraction, in which the same divisions are made for each application of the program. MOLGEN is more complex, in that it combines abstraction with a technique for generating the search space which may differ with each run.

8.2 R1

8.2.1 The Application

The objective of R1 is to take a list of system requirements for a VAX-11 computer system from the customer (as perceived by the salesman) and compute a working configuration of the components which make up the order. These are then output as a set of diagrams. The process therefore involves three interdependent activities: determining if the configuration is complete and making up any shortfall; forming a viable configuration; and producing a diagram of the appropriate spatial relationships between components.

R1 decides if a configuration is consistent from knowledge about individual components and the relationships between them. The VAX-11/780, for example, can be configured from over 400 components, each of which can have up to eight properties. This knowledge base therefore comprises over 3,000 pieces of component information. Successful spatial arrangements depend not only upon the above knowledge but also on further information related to the geometry of components and assemblies.

8.2.2 Control Structure

The system is a production system and is forward chained (data driven). There are three basic types of rule – sequencing rules, operator rules and information gathering rules. The first type divide the problem into a series of subtasks (or levels of abstraction). These are:

a) determine if there are any inconsistencies in the configuration;

b) put appropriate components into CPU cabinets;

c) put boxes in the unibus expansion cabinets and the appropriate components in the boxes;

d) put names in the unibus expansion cabinets;

e) lay out the system diagram;

f) work out the cabling.

This was the observed order in which configuration experts worked. For each subtask a context is set. Only those rules within that context can be fired. At the conclusion of a subtask a rule will generate a new context (that of the next subtask). No backtracking is necessary.

The operator rules check if components are to be treated in a special way (eg spares must not be configured). They check voltage and frequency levels, and that all required components are available. When placing components in cabinets, templates are used. Devices are allocated to adaptors and power supplies are configured. Modules are placed in the correct sequence on the unibus and required panel space is allocated. Backplanes are selected and modules placed in them. Panels are assigned to cabinets and associated with unibus modules. Finally a floor layout is generated.

The information gathering rules access the data base and carry out tasks to provide the sequencing and operator rules with appropriate information.

Enough knowledge is brought to bear at each step to determine which of the components should be configured next. Once a subtask is complete there is no need for any subsequent subtask to check if a previously configured component has in fact been configured correctly. The completion goal of each subtask is reached when no more rules can be applied. Although it would appear that the space is decomposable into a set of independent subtasks, this is not the case. Instantiations in earlier subtasks will affect instantiations in later subtasks. The consequences of any action are pushed into the unmatched part of the solution space but a later match can always be found. R1 thus uses a generalised form of matching.

Two examples of R1 rules are given below.

IF   The most current active context is putting unibus modules in backplanes in some box
    AND it has been determined which module to try to put in a backplane
    AND that module is a multiplexer terminal interface

AND it has not been associated with any panel space
AND the type and number of backplane slots it requires is known
AND there are at least that many slots available in a backplane of the
    appropriate type
AND the current unibus load on that backplane is known
AND the position of the backplane in the box is known

THEN Enter the context of verifying panel space for a multiplexer

IF   The most current active context is selecting a box and a module
    to put in it
AND the next module in the optimal sequence is known
AND the number of system units of space that the module requires is
    known
AND that box does not contain more modules than some other box on
    a different unibus

THEN Try to put that module in that box.

The first rule is a sequencing rule. It changes the context to "verifying panel space for a multiplexer". The second rule is an operator rule used for developing the configuration.

8.2.3 Knowledge Base

Each entry in the data base contains a description of a component, consisting of its name and a set of attribute-value pairs. Each component has a type and a class, recording the type of component (ie a disk drive) and the class of other relevant attributes (cabinet, sbi device, backplane, etc) present in the database. Figure 8.1 (taken from one of the R1 reports) shows a typical set of entries.

RK711-EA is a bundle of components. It contains a 25 foot cable (070-12292-25), a disk drive (RK07-EA*) and a bundle of components (RK611). RK07-EA* and RK611 are described also in Figure 8.1. These contain, amongst other things, the components RK611* and 070-12412-00 which are also shown.

The knowledge base also contains a set of templates which enable R1 to determine how full a particular component is at a particular time, and where to assign some other component to a specific location in it. A sample template for a cpu cabinet is shown in Figure 8.2.

RK711-EA
    Class: Bundle
    Type: Disk Drive
    Supported: Yes
    Component List: 1 070-12292-25
                 1 RK07-EA*
                 1 RK611
RK07-EA*
    Class: Unibus Device
    Type: Disk Drive
    Supported: Yes
    Floor Rank: 8
    Depth: 28 inches
    Width: 24 inches
    Height: 42 inches
    Unibus Module Required: RK611*
    Ports: 1
    Voltage: 120 volts
    Frequency: 60 hertz
    Cable Type Required: 1 070-12292 from a Disk Drive Unibus Module
                     or 1 070-12292 from a Disk Drive Unibus Device
RK611
    Class: Bundle
    Type: Disk Drive
    Supported: Yes
    Component List: 3 G727
                 1 M9202
                 1 070-12412-00
                 1 RK611*
070-12412-00
    Class: Backplane
    Type: RK611
    Supported: Yes
    Number of System Units: 2
    Length: 2.0 feet
    Number of Slots: 9
    Slot Types: 3 SPC (1 to 3)
              6 RK611 (4 to 9)
RK611*
    Class: Unibus Module
    Type: Disk Drive
    Supported: Yes
    Priority Level: Buffered NPR
    Transfer Rate: 212
    Number of System Units: 2
    Slots Required: 6 RK611 (4 to 9)
    Board List: (HEX A M7904) (HEX A M7903) (HEX A M7902) (HEX A M7901) (HEX A
       M7900)
    DC Power Drawn: 15.0 .175 .4
    Unibus Load: 1
    Number of Unibus Devices Supported: 8
    Cable Type Required: 1 070-12292 from a Disk Drive Unibus Device

Figure 8.1   Items in the Knowledge Base
(from McDermott J, *R1: A Rule-Based Configurer of Computer Systems*,
Carnegie-Mellon University Report CMU-CS-80-119, April 1980, p 8)

```
CPU-Cabinet
    Class: Cabinet
    Height: 60 inches
    Width: 52 inches
    Depth: 30 inches
    SBI Module Space: CPU Nexus–2 ( 3 5 23 30)
                      4-Inch-Option-Slot 1 Nexus-3 (23 5 27 30)
                      Memory Nexus-4 (27 5 38 30)
                      4-Inch-Option-Slot 2 Nexus-5 (38 5 42 30)
                      4-Inch-Option-Slot 3 Nexus-5 (42 5 46 30)
                      3-Inch-Option-Slot Nexus-6 (46 5 49 30)
    Power Supply Space: FPA Nexus-1 (2 32 10 40)
                        CPU Nexus-2 (10 32 18 40)
                        4-Inch-Option-Slot 1 Nexus-3 (18 32 26 40)
                        Memory Nexus-4 (26 32 34 40)
                        4-Inch-Option-Slot 2 Nexus-5 (34 32 42 40)
                        Clock-Battery (2 49 26 52)
                        Memory-Battery (2 46 26 49)
    SBI Device Space: IO (2 52 50 56)
```

Figure 8.2   A CPU Template

(from McDermott J, *R1: A Rule-Based Configurer of Computer Systems*, Carnegie-Mellon University Report CMU-CS-80-119, April 1980, p 10)

Figure 8.3 illustrates two rules, one of which is a subset of the other. The premises of the second rule are a special case of the first. The second rule will thus be chosen.

The height, width and depth are stated. A list of modules which may be ordered for the cabinet is then listed together with a description of how such modules may be fitted in. The knowledge base also contains knowledge about contexts, partial configurations, and the results of various sorts of computation.

R1 retrieves information from the base when it is needed either creating new components or extending existing ones.

8.2.4   Implementation

R1 was originally implemented in a production system language called OPS4 and relies upon a conflict resolution strategy used by OPS4. If two alternative instantiations are possible, it chooses the one which contains a proper subset of elements contained in the other. All rules are evaluated on every cycle.

The system was afterwards rewritten using OPS5, an improved version

Assign-Power-Supply-2

> IF: The most current active context is assigning a power supply
>   And an SBI module of any type has been put in a cabinet
>   And the position it occupies in the cabinet (its Nexus) is known
>   And there is space available in the cabinet for a power supply for that Nexus
>   And there is an available power supply
> THEN: Put the power supply in the cabinet in the available space

Assign-Power-Supply-6

> IF: The most current active context is assigning a power supply
>   And a Unibus adaptor has been put in a cabinet
>   And the position it occupies in the cabinet (its Nexus) is known
>   And there is space available in the cabinet for a power supply for that Nexus
>   And there is an available power supply
>   And there is no H7101 regulator available
> THEN: Add an H7101 regulator to the order

Figure 8.3   Conflict Resolution in R1
(from McDermott J, *R1: A Rule-Based Configurer of Computer Systems*,
Carnegie-Mellon University Report CMU-CS-80-119, April 1980, p 24)

of OPS4, which allows rules to be expressed in a more powerful way. The authors claim that OPS5 provides more intelligible rules. However, the rewrite into OPS5 provided an opportunity of evaluating the rules created so far and generalising them where possible. In the rewrite the original 750 rules were reduced to about 500. Only 50 of these were removed because of the improved representational capability of OPS5. Most of the reduction arose because of generalisation, the removal of redundancy and the simplification of configuring strategies.

The R1 project began late in 1978. The initial objective was to correctly configure 75% of orders, the 25% of failures being used to improve the rule set. R1 was given sample configurations and its output was checked by six independent experts. At the conclusion of the validation phase the experts were impressed with R1's performance so that it was decided to use R1 on a regular basis. In the following eight- month period, however, its performance was disappointing. The reason was traced to the way in which incomplete orders were dealt with. Apparently R1's technique of configuring "missing" components did not accord with traditional practice. The program was therefore modified to take this into account. Further developments increased the size of the rule set to 850. This growth illustrates the importance of incremental growth for knowledge-based systems. The new facilities which were added to R1 had not been envisaged in the prototype and yet were added without necessitating any significant change to existing rules.

By 1981 R1 was achieving a success rate in excess of 90% and it is now being extended to cover PDP11 configuring as well.

8.3 R1 CONCLUSIONS

McDermott has concluded that the initial choice of configuring VAX-11/780s was a fortunate one. It had just the right degree of difficulty. When the project was being formulated, PDP11 configuring was considered as an alternative starting point. If this had been chosen, McDermott has suggested that R1 would probably not have been adopted by DEC. The implementation of a knowledge-based system in an engineering environment is usually treated with a considerable amount of caution and scepticism. Repeatedly the knowledge engineers were disappointed at the levels of performance which had to be achieved to reduce this scepticism. At all times during the development of an expert system one has to maintain the support of the experts in the knowledge field of interest. Whilst R1's progress was slower than expected by the knowledge engineers, at no time did it consistently fail to reach realistic expectations. R1 survived because of the continued commitment of its supporters.

8.4 MOLGEN

8.4.1 The Task

The objective of MOLGEN is to assist biologists in designing experiments in molecular genetics. Since the interest is that of design, rather than analytical problem-solving, MOLGEN shares many of the problems of R1, the principal one being that it is not possible to completely specify goals at the start of a run. It is therefore not feasible to reduce the size of the search space by using some simple method such as "generate-and-test" because the construction of appropriate tests depends upon well specified goals. With incomplete specification there will always be a danger that a section of the search space will be prematurely pruned away, this area containing possible solutions based on information generated at some later stage of processing.

The solution to the search problem adopted in R1 was to abstract the design process, and then to order the abstracted task in such a way that each stage had clear goals and could be completed fully before the next stage was invoked. In this way, it was possible for the design task to be achieved, and to be accomplished without the need to undo any decisions previously made.

The control procedure employed by R1 is only applicable when the problem can be decomposed into a set of discrete stages which progressively home in sequentially through the levels of abstraction. However, this is not the case with the design of genetics experiments, it often not being possible to complete a sub-task until progress has been made in some other sub-task. In MOLGEN the set of tasks cooperate in parallel and are partially independent.

To illustrate this problem we may look at the design of a classic molecular genetics experiment which was taken as a model for MOLGEN – the rat-insulin experiment. This experiment concerns the use of bacteria for synthesising the hormone insulin, thus providing a better alternative to extracting it from the pancreas of animals. The experiment essentially involves splicing the gene coding for insulin production into bacteria thus causing the bacteria to produce insulin. This is achieved in a number of interacting stages, these being illustrated in Figure 8.4.

In order to get a culture of bacteria to produce insulin, it is necessary for the insulin gene code to be spliced into the organisms. However, this cannot be done directly, so an indirect method must be devised. This is the object of the experiment to be designed by MOLGEN. One possible indirect approach is to use a structure known as a "plasmid" which acts as a carrier to transport the gene into the bacteria. This process first requires the use of a restriction enzyme to cut open some plasmids, so that copies of the insulin gene can be inserted. The modified plasmids are then floated round the bacteria in solution, the bacteria absorbing them and thereby being transformed into insulin producers. Finally, the bacteria are allowed to reproduce in the presence of a "screening agent", which is an antibiotic chosen to eliminate all bacteria without the modified plasmids.

Although this "plan" may appear at first sight to be very simple, its execution requires a number of interactions between stages to be taken into account. These interactions are termed "constraints", and include the requirements that:

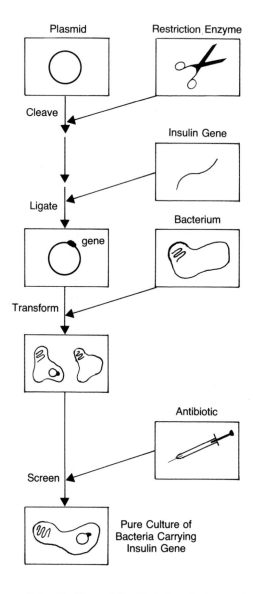

Figure 8.4   Outline of the Rat-Insulin Experiment
(from Stefik M J, *Planning with Constraints*, PhD Dissertation, 1980,
Heuristic Programming Project, Computer Science Department,
Stanford University, Stanford, CA)

i)   plasmids be selected which are capable of being absorbed by the bacteria;

ii) the bacteria should not be resistant to the antibiotic used in the final stage;

iii) the plasmids should make the bacteria resistant to the antibiotic;

iv) at the end of the process the resistance gene in the plasmids should still be intact, otherwise the modified bacteria will not be resistant to the antibiotic used for screening.

It should be noted that the above constraints are not stated explicitly as part of the MOLGEN goal. However, unless they are honoured the experiment will fail. It is thus necessary to identify them as processing proceeds and to find concrete solutions at each stage of the experimental design which obey them.

The problem of allowing for constraints during processing which only emerge during the course of a solution is a general characteristic of genetics experiments, whether they be analytic (concerned with determining the sequence of bases present in a DNA molecule) or synthetic (as in the above rat-insulin synthesis experiment). The system to be discussed here will be limited to the one designed by Stefik for synthetic tasks. Here the approach follows the principle of abstraction, planning for experiments being undertaken at three different levels. This is termed "meta-planning". Plans describing actual laboratory manipulations are made at the lowest level, the design of these plans is undertaken at the middle level and the strategy of design is undertaken at the highest level. At each level, individual problem-solving activities and, most importantly, interactions between them are represented explicitly, thus making them available to be reasoned about. As stated above, such interactions are termed "constraints".

8.4.2   A Sample MOLGEN Solution

Representation and processing in MOLGEN are sufficiently complex for it to be advantageous to approach the system by continuing with the example in more detail. Taking the rat-insulin experiment described above, MOLGEN is first presented with the very open-ended goal:

"we require an organism which is a bacterium which contains exosomes which are the vector carrying the genes which produce rat-insulin".

This is expressed in LISP as:

(Culture–1 with

    ORGANISMS: (BACTERIUM–1 with

        EXOSOMES: (VECTOR–1 with

           GENES: (RAT-INSULIN))))

BACTERIUM–1 and VECTOR–1 are variables. Following a very clear account given by Stefik, Figure 8.5 gives a pictorial representation used to describe goals in the figures employed to illustrate processing.

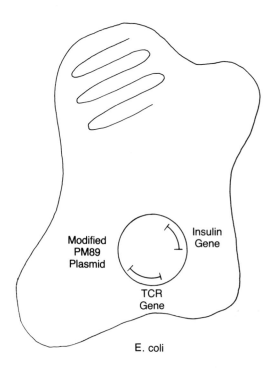

Figure 8.5   Representation of a Solution to the Rat-Insulin Experiment (from Stefik M J, *Planning with Constraints*, PhD Dissertation, 1980, Heuristic Programming Project, Computer Science Department, Stanford University, Stanford, CA)

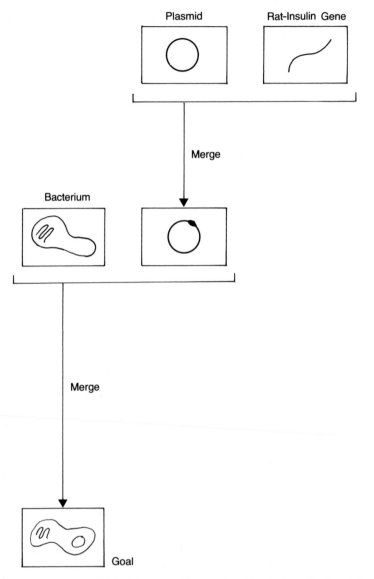

Figure 8.6   The Initial Abstract Plan Using the "Merge" Operator
(from Stefik M J, *Planning with Constraints*, PhD Dissertation, 1980,
Heuristic Programming Project, Computer Science Department,
Stanford University, Stanford, CA)

Figure 8.5 shows a specific type of bacterium – E.coli – which has absorbed a specific vector, a PM89 plasmid. This plasmid carries the insulin gene and a gene which gives resistance to the antibiotic tetracycline, TCR. The snake-like line at the top of the bacterium represents the bacterium chromosome.

Given the general goal statement, MOLGEN develops an abstract plan as illustrated in Figure 8.6. This states that a "Merge" operation should be employed first to combine the desired gene and a plasmid, and then to combine the transformed plasmid with a bacterium to form an insulin-producing bacterium.

Note that the details of the process are omitted at this stage. For example, it is not stated how the bacterium and plasmid are to be merged, or even which type of bacterium is to be used.

Having obtained an abstract plan, it is possible to refine it by selecting specific operators relating to laboratory operations. As these are introduced, they add constraints to the plan. This is illustrated in Figure 8.7. There are three planning actions involved, which are indicated by dashed arrows. The first action is to refine the Merge operator to the specific laboratory operator Transform, which itself requires the selection of a specific bacterium/plasmid combination (the Transform operator does not work for all pairs). However, MOLGEN does not want to make the choice at this stage because additional constraining factors may emerge later in processing. The system thus defers selection but "posts" the constraining fact that bacteria and transforming plasmids need to be compatible. This fact will be used later. The technique is known as "least commitment" and acts such that decisions lacking adequate constraints are delayed until more information is available. The posted constraint is represented in the figure as a dark box. Finally, MOLGEN simulates the Transform operator which mixes bacteria and plasmids together in solution, and finds that not all bacteria are transformed (see Figure 8.8).

The last step generates results which do not match the goal of transformation, some bacteria remaining which are not transformed. MOLGEN therefore proposes the abstract Sort operation to remove them, which is then refined to a specific Screen operator. It is found, however, that Screen uses an antibiotic and that this cannot be specified because the bacterium it is to operate upon has not itself been specified at this point. The antibiotic is thus left unspecified and remains represented in the system as an abstract variable.

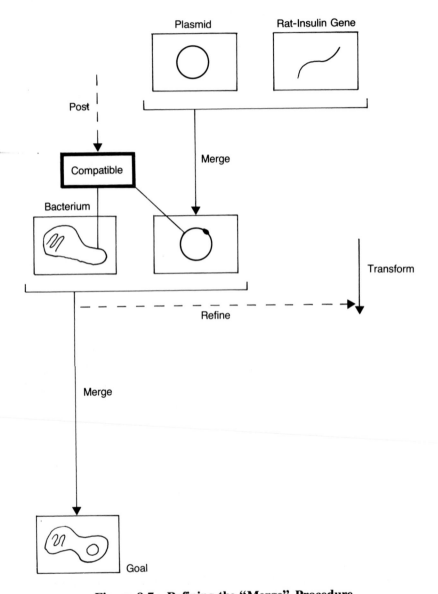

Figure 8.7 Refining the "Merge" Procedure
(from Stefik M J, *Planning with Constraints*, PhD Dissertation, 1980,
Heuristic Programming Project, Computer Science Department,
Stanford University, Stanford, CA)

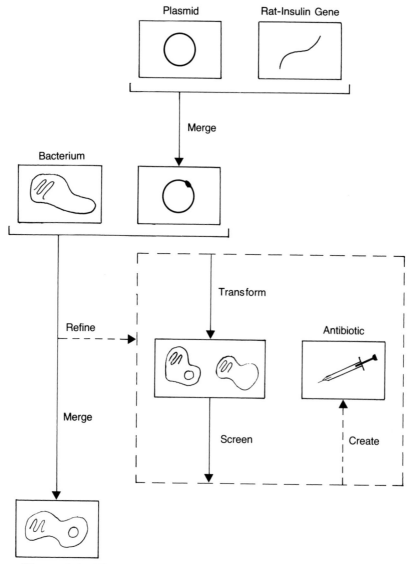

Figure 8.8   The Simulation of the Transform Operator and the Introduction of an Antibiotic

(from Stefik M J, *Planning with Constraints*, PhD Dissertation, 1980, Heuristic Programming Project, Computer Science Department, Stanford University, Stanford, CA)

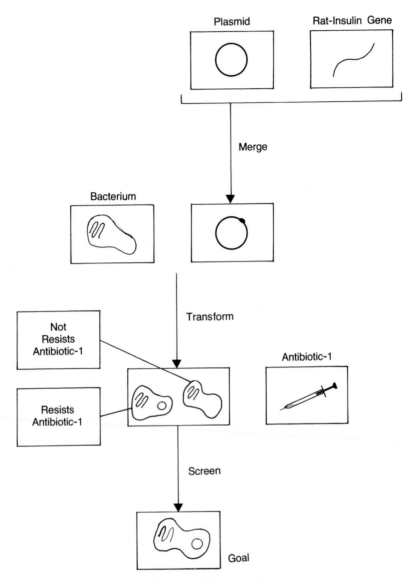

Figure 8.9   Constraints from the Screening Stage
(from Stefik M J, *Planning with Constraints*, PhD Dissertation, 1980,
Heuristic Programming Project, Computer Science Department,
Stanford University, Stanford, CA)

In order for Screening to be effective it is necessary that the untransformed bacteria be sensitive to the antibiotic while the transformed bacteria be able to resist it. However, as the actual bacteria and plasmids to be used remain unspecified, these constraints can only be posted (not satisfied).

The second operation involved in the experiment has now been refined to two specific laboratory operations: Transform and Screen. MOLGEN must attempt to refine the objects (the bacteria, plasmids and antibiotics) to be used by them. It may be recalled, however, that the first operator remains at its most abstract level, defined by a Merge operator. Moreover, this part of the problem is still "under-constrained" in that there are still many possible solutions. MOLGEN thus attempts to find additional constraints which will enable the step to be further refined. This is achieved through a process known as "constraint propagation".

MOLGEN notices that the bacteria input to the Transform stage are the same as those to be eliminated by screening, and thus should be sensitive to the antibiotic. The sensitivity constraint is therefore propagated backwards across the Transform step. Furthermore, it is noted that the bacteria intended to survive at the end of screening are identical to those named in the Screen goal and therefore must be resistant to the antibiotic. The resistance constraint is thus propagated forward across the Screen step. However, these are not the only possibilities for constraint propagation. The propagation of the resistance constraint backwards across the Transform step results in the requirement for a resistance gene in the plasmid, which is propagated as illustrated in Figure 8.10 to generate a new constraint.

With the new constraint on the choice of plasmid in place, MOLGEN switches attention to the initial Merge operation, temporarily abandoning the Screen step. The process continues in a similar manner to that described above, additional constraints being discovered, including the critical features concerning enzyme-recognition sites on the plasmid which are appropriately located with reference to the resistance gene.

8.4.3 Representation

The central structure of MOLGEN is represented explicitly as a three-level structure. Each of the levels is termed a "space". This structure is given in Figure 8.11.

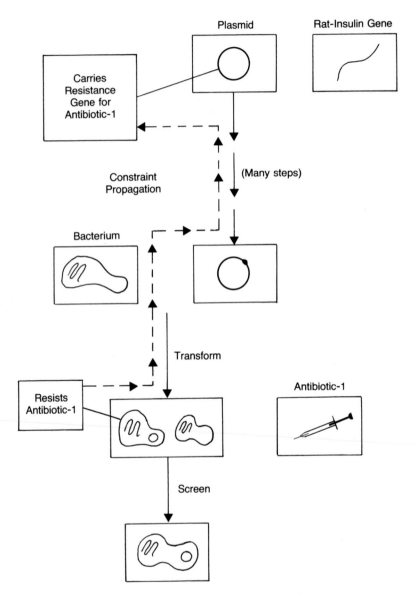

Figure 8.10 Constraint Propagation
(from Stefik M J, *Planning with Constraints*, PhD Dissertation, 1980,
Heuristic Programming Project, Computer Science Department,
Stanford University, Stanford, CA)

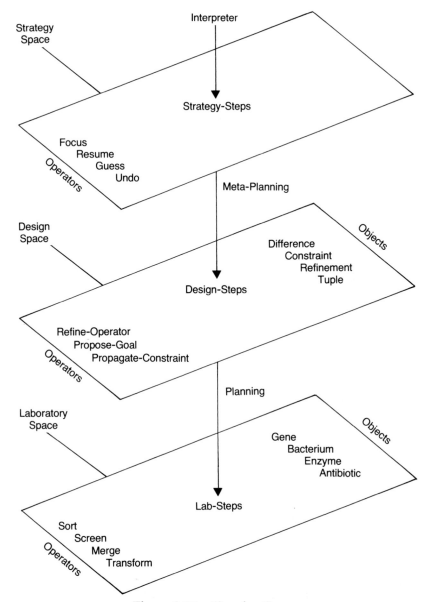

Figure 8.11 Planning Spaces
(from Stefik M J, *Planning with Constraints*, PhD Dissertation, 1980,
Heuristic Programming Project, Computer Science Department,
Stanford University, Stanford, CA)

The lowest level is termed the "laboratory space" and contains descriptions of the objects and operations (operators) used to conduct gene splicing experiments. These objects and operations are themselves described at various levels of abstraction. For example, at the lowest level there would be descriptions of specific bacteria and antibiotics such as E.coli or penicillin, whilst the highest level would contain the general terms "bacteria" and "drug". Operator and object knowledge at all levels of the system is described using a frame-type package known as "UNITS".

The middle MOLGEN planning area is termed the "design space", and is concerned with the development of plans at the laboratory level. Operations thus include planning activities such as laboratory operator refinement and constraint propagation, while objects include constraints and abstract entities such as "differences".

The top level of the planning space is concerned with "meta-planning". The principal strategy of MOLGEN is to use abstractions of object, operation and plans to avoid the need to undo any planning decision once made. However, this is not always possible, in which case it will be necessary to resort to some form of heuristic strategy allowing backtracking. The "strategy space" thus contains four very general operations:

— FOCUS and RESUME, which propose new planning steps and reactivate old ones that have been put on hold;

— GUESS and UNDO, which make heuristic planning decisions when there is not sufficient information to FOCUS or RESUME.

UNDO is a backtracking operator and GUESS is used to guess a task when no task can be identified by FOCUS and RESUME.

8.4.4 MOLGEN Reasoning

Taken together, the three planning areas of MOLGEN work together as a hierarchical control structure. The style of planning to be used is decided by the highest level. As discussed above, the two styles available are "least commitment" and "heuristic". The "least commitment" approach has priority because it provides for the most efficient planning, and proceeds in the following manner. MOLGEN first communicates with the experiment design operators in the design space (the middle space), asking for tasks to FOCUS upon. These include such activities as proposing a goal to be pursued or propagating a constraint. While undertaking one of these tasks, MOLGEN may find that it is unable to complete it because of lack of constraints. In this case the task will be "suspended", and another task sought. The situation may occur in which no new tasks can be found. MOLGEN responds by first re-examining all "suspended" tasks to see if any can be RESUMed, since additional constraints may have been created as a result of the fulfilment of other tasks. If no appropriate "suspended" tasks can be found, the top-level control space switches to the "heuristic" mode and GUESSes a plan.

Constraints in MOLGEN represent knowledge of interactions between sub-problems. They thus act as the chief means of communicating information on the course of problem-solution between sub-problems. There are three operations on constraints. The first, "constraint formulation", concerns the identification of such interactions. In section 8.4.2, for example, it was noted when refining the Merge operation of a bacterium and a plasmid into a Transform that the actual bacterium and plasmid selected had to be compatible for it to be successful. Not all plasmids will be absorbed by all bacteria.

The second operation concerns the generation of new constraints from old ones. This is termed "constraint propagation" and was illustrated in Figure 8.10. Here it was initially found that in order to screen bacteria which have been transformed by the modified plasmids from those which remain unchanged, the transformed bacteria must be resistant to the antibiotic used for screening. Having identified this fact, it is possible to make the simple inference that the plasmid used to make the transformation must carry a resistance gene for the antibiotic, since it is the plasmid which will carry out the transformation. This information may thus be attached as a constraint to govern the initial selection of the plasmid. The constraint is said to be propagated back across the Transform step to the plasmid variable.

Finally, at the close of the constraint propagation stage, MOLGEN seeks to "satisfy" constraints. This involves replacing an abstract object with a particular one which satisfies the constraint(s) put upon it.

8.5 MOLGEN CONCLUSIONS

MOLGEN follows in the tradition of DENDRAL in that it aims to provide the experimental scientist with automated assistance. It is intended that the MOLGEN project should provide a test-bed for such assistance. Moreover, the Stefik MOLGEN planner makes a valuable contribution to such systems in that the "least-commitment" strategy proves to be applicable to many design problems. Furthermore, it illustrates the power of providing different control strategies within the same system related in such a manner that the least expensive specialised control structure takes precedence but other more general structures are available to take over when it fails.

The Stanford MOLGEN project continues to explore the use of scientists' automated aids in molecular genetics. The project is now focusing upon a system called SPEX (Skeletal Planner of EXperiments) which combines many of the best features of Stefik's planner described above and an alternative system defined for planning analytical experiments built by Friedland. The hierarchical control structure employed by Stefik proved to cope well with the partial independence of sub-problems in experimental design. However, Stefik's system had the weakness of taking a long time to design reasonable experiments, especially when the degree of dependence was low. SPEX overcomes this by making use of more substantial domain knowledge.

9 Further Developments in Expert Systems

9.1 THE AUTOMATION OF PREDICATE LOGIC

In Chapter 3 we discussed the impasse reached in the automation of predicate logic. Whilst it was possible for a human logician to decide which rules of inference to apply to which particular propositions in order to conduct logical proofs, there appeared to be no obvious way of automating the process. Furthermore, because there was no way of effectively constraining inferences, an unconstrained approach would generate many uninteresting propositions rather than focusing upon some particular proposition to be proved.

Thus, the search for general problem-solving methods was abandoned, the more specific interest of automating problem-solving in specific areas being achieved by taking a programming approach using LISP, and concentrating upon issues of representing and using large bodies of domain specific knowledge. However, at the same time other workers, mainly in Europe, continued the search for a general solution to the automation of reasoning. This they eventually achieved and the result was a language called PROLOG.

The essential technique underlying PROLOG is termed "resolution theorem proving". The resolution technique solves the problems of inference rule selection and the generation of uninteresting propositions by reducing the proof procedure to the application of a single rule.

In order to apply the resolution principle (which will later be discussed in greater detail), sentences in predicate calculus are first reduced to a simplified notation termed "clausal form". This is possible because, as you may recall, all individual logical connectives may be re-expressed in terms of groups of other connectives. The simplification involves reducing an expression to a list of predicates connected by "ORs" (v). However, the implication connective used to express a rule (⟶) is later re-introduced in the PROLOG notation because some means of explicitly representing rules is important when predicate logic is to be used as a programming language.

9.1.1   Putting Predicate Calculus into Clausal Form

Casting a predicate calculus sentence into clausal form involves a process of simplification through transformation. To illustrate the sequence of transformations required we will work with a simple example:

"All computer scientists possess a password"

$\forall(X) \quad \exists(Y)$ (computer-scientist (X) $\rightarrow$ password (Y) possess (X,Y))

This can be read as meaning, for a particular computer scientist X, from the universal set of computer scientists, there exists a password Y, from the set of passwords, which X possesses.

If all variables in an expression are universally quantified, we can drop the universal quantifier. There is a problem, however, in the expression given above because the universal quantifier applies only to X and not to Y (ie all Ys do not satisfy the proposition). We solve this problem by introducing a function which generates at least one Y and uses X as its variable

eg comp-pass (X) $\equiv$ Y

This function is known as a Skolem function. We can now rewrite the expression

$\forall(X)$ (computer-scientist (X) $\rightarrow$ password (comp-pass (X)) & possess (X, comp-pass (X))

Now the universal quantifier applies to the whole expression and we can drop it.

The major hurdle is over. We now remove the "IMPLIES" connective using the rule that:

A $\rightarrow$ B is the same as $\sim$A v B

This converts the expression to:

~computer-scientist (X) v password (comp-pass (X)) & possess (X, comp-pass (X))

At this stage we have an expression which has the general form:

A v (B & C)

This expression actually contains two different "ORed" clauses:

A v B
A v C

and the clause can be written as:

~computer-scientist (X) v password (comp-pass (X))

~computer-scientist (X) v possess (X, comp-pass (X))

Expressed in English, the clauses state that

"If X is a computer-scientist THEN the password which is the value of the function 'comp-pass (X)', will be possessed by X".

Technically, the above statement of the proposition is said to be in "clausal form".

A logical sentence in clausal form is a series of propositions (or their negations) connected by OR

eg A v ~B v C v ~D

9.1.2 The Resolution Procedure

The basic operation underlying resolution is to cancel out propositions in different clauses when they are negated in one clause and unnegated in the other.

First we write down the facts we know in clausal form

1. ~B v A
2. C v B
3. ~C

Then we decide that we wish to prove A. To do this we add its negation to the set:

1. ~B v A   3. ~C
2. C v B   4. ~A

We now "cancel" this newly introduced clause with its negation in another clause. This is called resolution; eg we can cancel ~A in 4 with A in 1 leaving the remaining proposition (known as the "resolvent"), ie ~B. This leaves the clauses

1. ~B
2. C v B
3. ~C

Then we carry on, cancelling the resolvent ~B against B in clause 2 to leave

2. C
3. ~C

Finally these two cancel leaving the null clause [symbolised as ( )]. If a null clause can be achieved then the original proposition is proven. We are said to have achieved a "null resolvent".

We will now follow through the same reasoning using a concrete example. Let us assume we have the rule

computer-scientist (smith) → masochist (smith)

and the fact

computer-scientist (smith)

We are interested in seeing whether it could be concluded from this information that:

masochist (smith)

As described above, the assumptions are first cast into clausal form. Then the negation of the expected conclusion is introduced into the set, giving:

Clause 1   ~computer-scientist (smith) v masochist (smith)
Clause 2   computer-scientist (smith)
Clause 3   ~masochist (smith)

The resolution process may then proceed as follows (see Figure 9.1).

Two clauses are selected (C1 and C3 in this case) and the contradictory propositions are cancelled out to give a remainder – the "resolvent". Some other clause is then selected (C2) and is used with the resolvent to generate a second resolvent, which proves in this case to be the null

1. C3 : ~masochist (smith)   C1 : ~computer-scientist (smith) v masochist (smith)

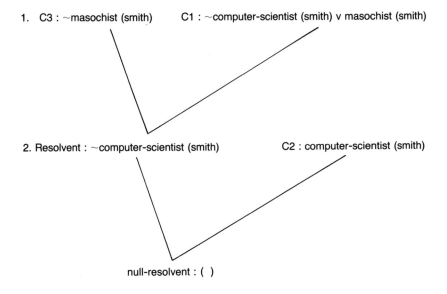

2. Resolvent : ~computer-scientist (smith)   C2 : computer-scientist (smith)

null-resolvent : ( )

Figure 9.1   Resolution Tree

clause. The generation of the null clause proves that the set of clauses contained a contradiction and, thus, we may conclude that the conclusion "masochist (smith)" is valid.

We now consider a slightly more complex argument, in which we wish to test that the fact

~growing (computer-science)

can be concluded from the rule and fact

growing (computer-science) → ~shortage (computer-science, applicants)

shortage (computer-science,applicants)

Put into clausal form, with the conclusion negated, we have:

Clause 1:   ~growing (computer-science) v ~shortage (computer-science,applicants)
Clause 2:   shortage (computer-science,applicants)
Clause 3:   growing (computer-science)

From inspection of Clause 3 it will readily be seen that resolving C3 against C1 will give the resolvent "~shortage (computer-science, applicants)" which will resolve against C2 to give a null clause. Hence, it may be concluded that "~growing (computer-science)".

At this point it is perhaps appropriate to ask how far we are towards automating predicate calculus. The answer is that with the clausal form of expression for propositions and with the resolution method we are close. The computer has a simple procedure to follow which prevents the combinatorial explosion mentioned at the end of Chapter 2 (where uninteresting propositions were generated by the repeated blind application of a rule such as "& inclusion"). However, the resolution method does not itself indicate which clauses are to be selected for resolution. In the examples there was no real problem because there were so few clauses but with only a modest increase we stumble upon a second type of combinatorial explosion. If we tried all combinations of clauses, it has been estimated by Charniak that with 10 clauses there will be over 50 possibilities on the first try at resolution, rising to about 10^{17} possibilities by the 10th try. To illustrate the impossibility of employing such a system without some means of limiting the explosion, there are less than 10^{10} seconds in a century.

The problem with the resolution technique as it has been described is that it lacks an appropriate control structure to prevent the combinatorial explosion. Several different methods have been devised, many of them not proving very satisfactory. However, recently a reasonably efficient method has been found that has given rise to the logic programming language PROLOG.

9.1.3   PROLOG and Programming in Logic

In order to develop a programming language out of the application of resolution theorem proving to predicate calculus, the "IMPLIES" connective is in effect re-introduced into the clausal syntax. It will be recalled that a logical expression in clausal form consists of propositions (or their negations) connected by ORs. Any set of propositions connected by ORs can be re-arranged without change of meaning. The first step is therefore to separate out the negated propositions on the left and the unnegated on the right, eg

$$A \vee {\sim}B \vee C \vee {\sim}D \vee {\sim}E$$

is written as

$(\sim B \lor \sim D \lor \sim E) \lor (A \lor C)$

We now use the fact that a set of ORed negated propositions can be written as a negated set of ANDed propositions, eg

$(\sim B \lor \sim D \lor \sim E) \equiv \sim(B \,\&\, D \,\&\, E)$

Our sentence then becomes

$\sim(B \,\&\, D \,\&\, E) \lor (A \lor C)$

We now transform this to the "IMPLIES" form by using the fact that

$\sim G \lor H \equiv G \rightarrow H$

so our sentence becomes

$B \,\&\, D \,\&\, E \rightarrow A \lor C$

In other words a set of ANDed conditions imply an ORed set of conclusions. We are now almost ready to cast the sentence into the programming language PROLOG. We introduce a further restriction, that each clause may only have a single conclusion. The above clause would then have to be written as

$B \,\&\, D \,\&\, E \rightarrow A$
$B \,\&\, D \,\&\, E \rightarrow C$

These are called "Horn clauses".

To make the sentence clear the order in PROLOG is actually reversed

Conclusion $\leftarrow$ Conditions

which in standard PROLOG notation is written as

Conclusion :– Conditions

or for our example

A :– $B \,\&\, D \,\&\, E$
C :– $B \,\&\, D \,\&\, E$

The reader will also notice that our formal notation in Chapter 1 corresponds with the above, ie

Clause 1:   manages (peter,john):–

Clause 2:   manages (john,ann):–
Clause 3:   manages (ann,fred):–
Clause 4:   reports-to (X,Y):– manages (Y,X)
Clause 5:   reports-to (X,Z):– manages (Z,Y) & reports-to (X,Y)

Note that a fact is represented as an unconditional conclusion

manages (peter,john):–

A query (that which we wish to prove) is negated in accordance with the resolution technique, ie ?– A becomes ~ A. Since ~ A v B is A → B (or B :– A) then ~ A is A → (or :– A). So a query is a condition or set of conditions without a conclusion.

A query in PROLOG is thus addressed as

:– reports-to (fred,peter)

The problem in PROLOG is to decide which two clauses should be resolved against each other. This requires some form of control structure. The control process used by PROLOG is best understood using the concept of a state-space search introduced in Chapter 3 and employed throughout our discussion of expert systems. Propositions within a set of related PROLOG clauses may be represented as a hierarchically organised search space (as an "AND/OR tree"). This may be appreciated most readily if we take an abstract example (Figure 9.2).

Inspection of Figure 9.2 will reveal that the body of the tree is formed from inter-related rules, with the facts occupying terminal positions. Furthermore, it will be recalled that within PROLOG the conditions of a rule are "ANDed" branches. Where the same conclusion may be reached from different conditions, the conditions are read as being "ORed", in which case the branches are drawn with no link between them.

A PROLOG AND/OR tree may be read both declaratively, as is the convention in logic, or procedurally, as is conventional in programming. For example, following logic we can assert that for the proposition "p" to be "true", *both* "q" and "r" must be "true", and for "q" to be true *either* "s" or "t" must be "true". Given a procedural reading, the PROLOG rules can be interpreted as decomposing the proof of a given proposition. The proof of "p" decomposes into the proof of "q" and "r", while the proof of "q" decomposes into either the proof of "s" or "t".

```
C1 p : - q & r
C2 q : - s
C3 q : - t
C4 r : - a & b
C5 s : -
C6 a : -
C7 b : -
```

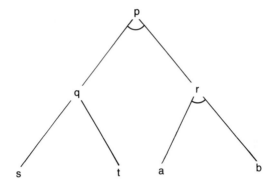

Figure 9.2   AND/OR Tree for a Simple Abstract Program

Given the representation of a set of PROLOG clauses as an AND/OR tree, it is possible to consider various strategies for traversing it. This is equivalent to producing a strategy for deciding which clauses to select for resolution in resolution theorem proving. The strategy adopted by PRO-LOG is to traverse the tree depth-first, starting from the left. Let us assume with the present example that we wish to prove the proposition "p". This would be expressed as a negated form as:

$$:-p$$

and it would be added to the set of clauses in the normal way. In PROLOG terminology the query proposition(s) is termed a "goal". This goal ":–p" is then "matched" against the first clause that has "p" as its conclusion. In the present case there is only one "p:– q&r". PROLOG then takes the first conditional assumption it comes across – "q" – and seeks to prove this to be true. Being a condition, it is already negated and so may simply be set as a new goal – or "subgoal" – and "matched" against the first clause with the conclusion "q" – a conclusion is known as the "head" of a clause in PROLOG. This process will continue in the present case until the subgoal ":–s" is created and matched against the fact "s". Thus the proposition "s" has been proved true. Having "satisfied" "q" via "s", PROLOG can now start work at "r" which is satisfied first via "a" and then via "b". Thus the original query ":–p" is proved by traversing the following sequence of nodes in the tree: p, q, s, r, a, b. It should be noted that if it had not been possible to prove "q" or "r" due to the absence of any of "s", "t", "a" or "b" from the program, then the query ":–q" would have failed (to have been proved).

There is an additional feature of PROLOG execution which needs to be explained. When PROLOG came to match the "subgoal" ":–q" in the above exposition, it selected the head of the first clause with "q" as its condition. Having satisfied "q" (via the satisfaction of "s"), it proceeded to seek a match for the new subgoal "r". However, this raises the question of what would have happened if the two "q" clauses had been in the other order, with "q:–t" coming first? PROLOG uses "backtracking" to cope with this situation. The relevant AND/OR tree is given in Figure 9.3.

Let us assume that the same query , ":–p" , is addressed to the system as before. The goal ":–p" will match the head "p" and generate the subgoal ":–q". This will match the head "q", generating the subgoal ":–t", which will fail, there being no "t". Given this failed match, the system will "backtrack" to find the last successful match and then seek some alterna-

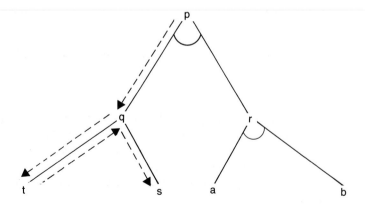

Figure 9.3   AND/OR Tree to Illustrate Backtracking

tive. This it will find in the second clause with "q" at its head – "q:–s". The proof may then proceed as before.

Our final example is given to illustrate the details of PROLOG execution. In this case we have chosen to use more realistic PROLOG clauses which contain variables. Moreover, the clauses are so ordered that the interpreter will need to backtrack during execution. The clauses are:

C1:   likes (jill,wine)
C2:   likes (john,food)
C3:   likes (john,wine)
C4:   male (john)
C5:   escort (X,Y) :– likes (Y,wine) & male (Y)

The tree representation of the single rule would be as in Figure 9.4.

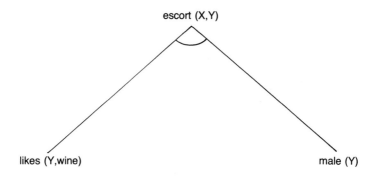

Figure 9.4   Tree Representation of a Single Rule

Even with a program as simple as this, execution may appear quite complex. To clarify the process we have a special notation termed a goal tree. This gives a trace of the matching attempted between clause heads, goals and subgoals, along with a record of the results. A goal tree for our program is given in Figure 9.5, following the query ":–escort (mary,X1)", ie "Who is Mary's escort?".

Matching on the "escort" clause, X is instantiated with the value "Mary". Passing right into the conditions, we get a new goal "likes (Y,

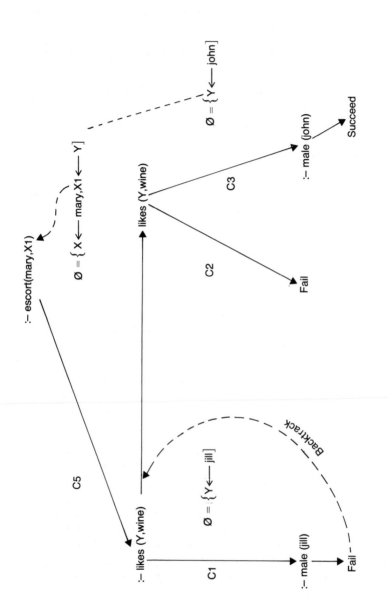

Figure 9.5   **Trace of PROLOG Execution**

wine)", which matched the first assertion "likes (jill,wine"). We then pass on the ANDed condition, generating the new query "male (jill)", which fails. PROLOG then backtracks to find an alternative instantiation for "Y", which it finds in the third assertion with "john". The new goal "male (john)" is now generated, which succeeds. This gives us a value for "X1", namely "john". The whole query thus now succeeds, the original query being unified with the "escort" clause taking the value of "john" for "X1".

9.2 SOME ADVANTAGES OF PREDICATE LOGIC

The use of predicate logic as a programming language has a number of advantages. Most of these derive from logic rather than the control structures used to automate the logic. Indeed, most of the disadvantages of a logic programming language such as PROLOG follow from the control techniques.

First, logic provides a well established representational formalism which is clear, has an agreed interpretation in natural English and which can easily handle issues of quantification. This is often a problem with pragmatic forms of representation, most notably semantic networks. In this case, the problem of semantic networks has been solved with the notation of partitioned networks but it periodically reappears as other specialised forms of representation are developed to cope with some specific subject material. Secondly, advantages arise from the deductive procedures of predicate calculus. The use of formal rules of inference in logical argument enables conclusions to be guaranteed, where they can be drawn, and provides a mechanism to trace the source of their failure, where they may not be drawn.

The latter procedure has been applied to the problem of keeping databases of facts consistent. Here the approach involves maintaining a record of the conditions (termed "beliefs") which lead to conclusions. This record of beliefs can then be used for such purposes as tracking down the conclusions which no longer hold with some change in assumptions and tracing the source of a contradiction when it is found to occur. The above procedures are termed "truth maintenance" and they begin to explore some of the "non-monotonic" aspects of reasoning which we mentioned at the end of Chapter 2.

The problem of automating non-monotonic reasoning was discussed at the end of Chapter 2. It may be recalled that, in a monotonic system, conclusions never have to be withdrawn with the addition of facts. However, this is not true of much human reasoning, it often being necessary to revise conclusions in the light of new facts. In computer programming, this situation is handled by means of "default values" (Chapter 3, sections 3.3.1 and 3.3.2), it being assumed that some fact or value is true unless some alternative is explicitly computed. While it is possible to set up appropriate defaults for some restricted application, no widely accepted system for processing logic defaults is available. As a result, it is not possible to devise a logic programming language which automatically handles defaults in a totally general way. This is an important current topic of research.

There are, of course, some limits to the expressive power of predicate calculus, at least to that which may be expressed within its classical formal limits, for example, the expression of possibilities, intentions, beliefs, etc. However, with an automated form it is possible to use logic as a programming language and to implement functionally equivalent heuristics where no formal processes are available.

The control aspect of PROLOG, as a particular implementation of automated logic, is less satisfactory. The standard form of PROLOG uses a single control structure which may be described as a top-down depth-first search with backtracking. In theory, this technique is sufficiently general not to complicate thinking about problems. It is thus intended that issues of control should be largely ignored by the programmer, who is then free to solve his problem in declarative terms. In practice, however, this is not so simple.

One important difficulty is that the procedural aspect of PROLOG puts a non-logical constraint on clauses concerning their order. With an inappropriate ordering, some undesired deductions may be made which are logically correct but which do not satisfy the programmer's objectives. To avoid this problem, the programmer needs to be willing on certain occasions to consider PROLOG programs in procedural terms. However, the process of PROLOG execution may often be difficult to understand, being ill supported by the syntax of the language. Moreover, this obscurity is further heightened by the "backtracking" aspect of control.

A final problem concerns the implementation of programs with control structures which differ from the base system of a "depth-first search". The execution of a "breadth-first search", for example, is less efficient programmed in PROLOG than in a language with more primitive control structures, eg PASCAL. Furthermore, such PROLOG programs may be hard to understand and debug because of interference in the programmer's mind between the two types of control structure. The backward chaining aspect of PROLOG creates similar difficulties if one wishes to program a forward chained system.

9.3 DEVELOPMENTS IN EXPERT SYSTEMS

The previous sections have considered the possible use of predicate logic as a programming language and the advantages of such a language. Developments in this direction are currently being undertaken within European Artificial Intelligence and in Japan as part of the 5th generation computer development. There is also interest in the United States in logic programming, although as more of an extension of LISP than as the basic programming vehicle. Logic programming is not the only source of development, however. Other areas include:

— the extension of expert systems to employ forms of knowledge other than simple empirical associations and the design of architectures to support them;

— the design of systems to undertake a wider range of cognitive functions than the largely predetermined, system directed problem-solving of earlier programs.

Much recent research has been undertaken into the use of so called "deep knowledge" for expert systems. The term "deep knowledge" includes models of the functional and causal relations that underlie a problem, problem-solving being based on these rather than upon empirical associations.

One of the principal advantages of using functional and causal knowledge is that the reasons behind a given course of inference may be more readily made explicit. This was illustrated in Chapter 6 when we discussed the CASNET system. It may be recalled, for example, that diagnostic questions were clearly motivated by the need to establish successive stages in a disease process. The model of the disease process thus forms the explanation for the order of questioning and the diagnostic solution may itself be justified by disease processes established during the session.

Systems using functional and causal models have been developed using a variety of representations. These range from systems which "compile" the causal relations required to undertake a particular class of problem-solving (eg diagnosis, database retrieval), to systems which execute problem-solving procedures on relational models of the problem domain. It is claimed with reference to "compiled" systems that it is possible to undertake all of the inference and explanation operations that would be possible with the explicit representation of causal knowledge.

Other work using explicit causal models has concentrated on their adequacy to solve particular classes of problem. Research on the design of a system for diagnosing faults in electronic circuits has, for example, indicated that implicit within any causal model are assumptions concerning the scope of possible causal interactions. The effectiveness of a particular model will be determined in part by these assumptions. If the models are to be used in a diagnostic system, certain faults will imply variations in interactions. It may thus be necessary to entertain an ordered set of models of increasing complexity, each capable of identifying different classes of fault. To reduce the size of the search space, which may be prohibitively large if all possible interactions are included, successive models need to be available for exploration as lower level models are proved to be inadequate.

The second set of developments concern extending the range of cognitive activities undertaken by expert systems. Traditional expert systems have been narrowly concerned with problem-solving. The priority for designers has been that systems should be capable of producing accurate and exact solutions to a problem; it was not of central importance that the system did so using similar methods to those used by human experts. While it was desirable that the system be capable of explaining its reasoning, systems were not designed with this in mind and were optimised for reasoning effectiveness rather than coherence. Explanation facilities gave more attention to answering questions concerning the abstract inference processes used by the system than attempting to explain reasoning with direct reference to the problem domain. Furthermore, explanation facilities were not intended to attack in detail the problem of making reasoning understandable to a particular user with particular background knowledge and understanding problems.

Individual cognitive functions (eg problem-solving, learning) rarely take place in isolation. It is usual for them to be interrelated when applied to a task of any complexity. When faced with computer support for such a task, any individual function will need to be augmented by some "user complement" of additional cognitive functions. The history of the use of computer aids suggests that support of these additional functions is usually requested eventually. Initial attempts at this often employ the same knowledge base, although this is usually not well adapted to other functions. This stage is then followed by the re-design of the initial system to accommodate the additional requirements.

The above sequence exactly mirrors the development of expert systems. The primary emphasis was upon effective problem-solving. However, the complexity of processing in many knowledge-based systems was such that some "explanation facility" was required to enable reasoning to be evaluated and debugged. The use of the primitive explanation facilities such as those found in MYCIN or PROSPECTOR suggested alternative roles for systems which fitted the application context more comfortably than originally conceived in the design of the system. Adapting systems to such roles is motivating the design of alternative architectures.

The adaptation of a conventional system to alternative roles may be illustrated with reference to MYCIN. One of the early extensions was to attempt to use MYCIN to teach diagnosis – the GUIDON system. However, it was found that more was required than the simple addition of rules to govern teaching strategy and student modelling. The basic MYCIN knowledge base was found to be inadequate for teaching purposes, lacking the requisite explicit knowledge of the primitives of the domain (eg the fact that E.coli is a bacterium) and the structure of the domain (eg a taxonomy of bacterial infections). This type of knowledge eases the task of learning.

Experiments such as the above have indicated that knowledge-based systems emphasising educational functions will be differently structured from problem-solving systems. It is, however, possible to maintain the problem-solving orientation while allowing the system itself to learn from "experience". This is illustrated by the SHRINK system for aiding psychiatric diagnosis. This system draws upon architectures used by natural language understanding systems, in particular the concept of a "failure-driven memory", to recognise when its reasoning has failed and to take remedial action to modify its factual or inferential knowledge to correct the failure.

A further role undertaken by knowledge-based systems, which amounts to an extension of the expert system concept rather than a radical departure in cognitive function, is that of critically evaluating the user's reasoning. The system acts to shadow the user and interrupts when a significant discrepancy is found. One example of such a system is the most recent version of ONCOCIN which was developed by the MYCIN group to record and critique plans for the chemical treatment of cancer.

Finally, a number of developments should be mentioned which are taking place within the main area of expert systems. First, research is being conducted in using multiple sources of knowledge where it is not possible to adopt some simpler approach. The classic example of the use of this approach is in the HEARSAY-11 system used in speech understanding. Here information ranging from the parameters of the speech signal to semantic context are available, and each in itself may be unable to interpret an utterance. However, used co-operatively one may serve where the other fails. Secondly, work is being conducted into establishing a more formal basis for expert systems. A notable piece of work in this area applies the mathematical theory of set covering to medical diagnosis. This approach provides a solution to the difficult problem of multiple simultaneous disorders, which is also tackled programmatically by INTERNIST, but provides the mathematical basis for determining the validity of a solution.

Expert systems have now reached a critical stage in their development. The early research has established the viability of the approach. What is now needed is an extensive phase of critical evaluation of their use in real environments.

Bibliography

CHAPTER 1

Barr A & Feigenbaum E A (eds) (1981), *The Handbook of Artificial Intelligence*, Vols I & II, Los Altos, CA: Kaufmann.

Cohen P R & Feigenbaum E A (eds) (1982), *The Handbook of Artificial Intelligence*, Vol III, Los Altos, CA: Kaufmann.

Hayes-Roth F, Waterman D A & Lenat D (eds) (1983), *Building Expert Systems*, Reading, MA: Addison Wesley.

Webber B L & Nilsson N J (eds) (1981), *Readings in Artificial Intelligence*, Palo Alto, CA: Tioga Press.

Winston P H (1977), *Artificial Intelligence*, Reading, MA: Addison-Wesley.

CHAPTER 2

Hodges W F (1978), *Logic*, Harmondsworth: Penguin Press.

Lemmon E J (1972), *Beginning Logic*, London: Nelson.

CHAPTER 3

Brackman R J (1979), On the epistemological status of semantic networks. In N V Findler (ed), *Associative Networks: Representation and Use of Knowledge by Computers*, London: Academic Press.

Bundy A, Burstall R M, Weir S & Young R M (1978), *Artificial Intelligence: An Introductory Course*, Edinburgh: Edinburgh University Press.

Davis R (1982), *Expert Systems: Where are We? and Where do We Go from Here?*, AI Memo No 665, MIT AI Laboratory.

Davis R & King J (1976), An overview of production systems. In E W Elcock & D Michie (eds), *Machine Intelligence*, 8, New York: Wiley.

Gloess P Y (1981), *Understanding Artificial Intelligence*, Sherman Oaks, CA: Alfred Publishing Co.

Haugeland J (1981), Semantic engines: an introduction to mind design. In J Haugeland (ed), *Mind Design: Philosophy, Psychology and Artificial Intelligence*, Montgomery, VT: Bradford Books.

Hendrix G G (1979), Encoding knowledge in partitioned networks. In N V Findler (ed), *Associative Networks: Representation and Use of Knowledge by Computers*, London: Academic Press.

Minsky M L (1980), A framework for representing knowledge. In J Haugeland (ed), *Mind Design: Philosophy, Psychology, and Artificial Intelligence*, Montgomery, VT: Bradford Books.

Nilsson N J (1982), *Principles of Artificial Intelligence*, New York: Springer-Verlag.

Norman D, Rumelhart D E & the LNR Group (1975), *Explorations in Cognition*, San Francisco: W H Freeman and Co.

Winston P H & Horn B K P (1981), *LISP*, Reading, MA: Addison-Wesley.

Woods W A (1975), What's in a link: foundations of semantic networks. In D G Bobrow & A Collins (eds), *Representation and Understanding: Studies in Cognitive Science*, London: Academic Press.

CHAPTER 4

Schank R & Abelson R (1977), *Scripts, Plans, Goals and Understanding*, Hillsdale, NJ: Lawrence Erlbaum.

Sleeman D & Brown J S (eds) (1982), *Intelligent Tutoring Systems*, London: Academic Press.

Stefik M, Aikins J, Balzer R, Beniot J, Birnbaum L, Hayes-Roth F & Sacerdoti E (1982), *The Organization of Expert Systems: A Prescrip-*

tive Tutorial, Research Report VLSI-82-1, XEROX PARC, Palo Alto, CA.

CHAPTER 5

Davis R (1983), TEIRESIAS: Experiments in communication with a knowledge-based expert system. In M E Sime & M J Coombs (eds), *Designing for Human-Computer Communication*, London: Academic Press.

Davis R & Lenat D B (1982), *Knowledge-Based Systems in Artificial Intelligence*, New York: McGraw-Hill.

Duda R O, Gaschnig J & Hart P E (1979), Model design in the PROS-PECTOR consultant program for mineral exploration. In D Michie (ed), *Expert Systems in the Microelectronic Age*, Edinburgh: Edinburgh University Press.

Duda R O, Gaschnig J, Hart P E, Konolige K, Reboh R, Barrett P & Slocum J (1978), *Development of the PROSPECTOR Consultation System for Mineral Exploration*, Final Report, SRI Projects 5821 and 6451, SRI International Inc, Menlo Park, CA.

Duda R O, Hart P E & Nilsson N (1976), *Subjective Bayesian Methods for Rule-Based Inference Systems*, Proceedings of the National Computer Conference, AFIPS, 45, 1075-1082.

Shortliffe E H (1976), *Computer-Based Medical Consultations: MYCIN*, New York: American Elsevier.

Shortliffe E H & Buchanan B G (1975), A model of inexact reasoning in medicine, *Mathematical Bioscience*, 23, 351-379.

CHAPTER 6

Kulikowski C A & Weiss S M (1982), Representation of expert knowledge for consultation: the CASNET and EXPERT projects. In P Szolovitz (ed), *Artificial Intelligence in Medicine*, Boulder, Colorado: Westview Press.

Miller A M, Pople H E & Myers J D (1982), INTERNIST-I, an experimental computer-based diagnostic consultant for general internal medicine, *New England Journal of Medicine*, 307, 468-476.

Pople H E (1977), The formation of composite hypotheses in diagnostic problem solving: an exercise in synthetic reasoning, *Proceedings of the 5th International Joint Conference in Artificial Intelligence*, Carnegie-Mellon University, Pittsburgh.

Pople H E (1982), Heuristic methods for imposing structure on ill-structured problems: the structuring of medical diagnostics. In P Szolovitz (ed), *Artificial Intelligence in Medicine*, Boulder, Colorado: Westview Press.

Weiss S M, Kulikowski C A, Amaral S & Safir A (1978), A model-based method for computer-aided medical decision-making, *Artificial Intelligence*, 11, 145-172.

CHAPTER 7

Buchanan B G & Feigenbaum E A (1978), DENDRAL and Meta-DENDRAL: the applications dimension, *Artificial Intelligence*, 11, 5-24.

Buchanan B G, Smith D H, White W C, Gritter R, Feigenbaum E A, Lederberg J & Djerassi C (1976), Applications of artificial intelligence for chemical inference. XXII. Automatic rule formation in mass spectrometry by means of the meta-DENDRAL program, *Journal of the American Chemical Society*, 96, 6168.

Buchanan B G, Sutherland G L & Feigenbaum E A (1969), Heuristic DENDRAL: a program for generating explanatory hypotheses in organic chemistry. In B Meltzer & D Michie (eds), *Machine Intelligence*, 4, Edinburgh: Edinburgh University Press.

Buchanan B G, Sutherland G L & Feigenbaum E A (1970), Towards an understanding of information processes of scientific inference in the context of organic chemistry. In B Meltzer & D Michie (eds), *Machine Intelligence*, 5, Edinburgh: Edinburgh University Press.

Lindsay R K, Buchanan B G, Feigenbaum E A & Lederberg J (1980), *Applications of Artificial Intelligence in Organic Chemistry: The DENDRAL Project*, New York: McGraw-Hill.

CHAPTER 8

Friedland P E (1979), *Knowledge-Based Experiment Design in Molecular*

Genetics, PhD Dissertation, Heuristic Programming Project, Computer Science Department, Stanford University, Stanford, CA.

McDermott J (1980), *R1: A Rule-Based Configurer of Computer Systems*, Research Report CMU-CS-80-119, Department of Computer Science, Carnegie-Mellon University, Pittsburgh, PA.

McDermott J (1981), R1's formative years, *AI Magazine*, 2.

McDermott J (1982), EXCEL: a computer salesperson's assistant. In J Hayes, D Michie & Y -H Pao (eds), *Machine Intelligence*, 10, Chichester: Ellis Horwood.

Stefik M J (1980), *Planning with Constraints*, PhD Dissertion, Heuristic Programming Project, Computer Science Department, Stanford University, Stanford, CA.

CHAPTER 9

Chandrasekaran B & Mittal S (1984), Deep versus compiled approaches to diagnostic problem-solving. In M J Coombs (ed), *Developments in Expert Systems*, London: Academic Press.

Clancey W J (1983), The epistemology of a rule-based expert system: a framework for explanation, *Artificial Intelligence*, 20, 215-251. [GUIDON]

Clocksin W F & Mellish C (1981), *Programming in Prolog*, Heidelberg, West Germany: Springer-Verlag.

Davis R (1984), Reasoning from first principles in electronic troubleshooting. In M J Coombs (ed), *Developments in Expert Systems*, London: Academic Press.

Davis R & Lenat D B (1982), *Knowledge-Based Systems in Artificial Intelligence*, New York: McGraw-Hill.

Doyle J (1979), A truth maintenance system, *Artificial Intelligence*, 12, 231-272.

Kolodner J L (1984), Towards an understanding of the role of experience in the evolution from novice to expert. In M J Coombs (ed), *Developments in Expert Systems*, London: Academic Press. [SHRINK]

Kowalski R (1979), *Logic for Problem Solving*, New York: Elsevier/ North Holland.

Langlotz C P & Shortliffe E H (1984), Adapting a consultation system to critique user plans. In M J Coombs (ed), *Developments in Expert Systems*, London: Academic Press. [ONCOCIN]

Lenat D B & Harris G (1978), Designing a rule system which searches for scientific discoveries. In D A Waterman & F Hayes-Roth (eds), *Pattern-Directed Inference Systems*, New York: Academic Press.

Reggia J A, Nau D S & Wang P Y (1984), Diagnostic expert systems based on a set covering model. In M J Coombs (ed), *Developments in Expert Systems*, London: Academic Press.

Index

abstraction   92, 153-155, 162
 (*see also* control)
argument, logical   38, 39, 40, 41
array   24, 25
Artificial Intelligence 19, 37, 51, 53, 57, 76, 81,
         85, 87, 90, 137, 153, 191

associative memory
 (*see* semantic network)
associative network
 (*see* semantic network)

backtracking   23, 36, 56, 154, 156
 (*see also* search)
backward-chaining 94, 95, 99
 (*see also* production system)
BASIC   24
Bayes' Theorem   110-111
beliefs   189
bottom-up inference 78-79, 128, 134

CADUCEUS   120, 128
 (*see also* INTERNIST)
CASNET   86, 88, 120, 129-135
 – causal knowledge 91, 129-130
 – conclusions   134-135
 – diagnostic strategy 129-130, 133-134

– inexact inference   130, 133
– representation   130-133
– semantic network   91, 129, 130-133
causal knowledge   91, 129-130
 (*see also* CASNET)
classes, logical   17-21, 24-26, 28-29, 64
CLOT   94
COBOL   24, 25
combinatorial explosion   50, 80, 182, 192
constants, representation of   19-20, 40
constraints   145, 149, 162, 164, 167,
                                       171, 174, 175
– formulation   175
– propagation   171, 174, 175
 (*see also* control)
context tree   98, 99
contextual relations   115
control   76-82
– abstraction   92, 153-155, 162
– constraints   145, 149, 162-167, 171-175
– domain dependence   31-33, 82, 85, 94, 99
– generate-and-test   91-92, 137-138, 153, 154,
                                       161
– knowledge-based   53-57
– least commitment   92, 167, 174, 176
– operator   78, 155, 167, 171, 174-175
– state-space search   76-82, 89
– structure   21-23, 27, 55-57

data base management systems   19
data-directed searching   96
data-driven system   27-28, 97
data processing, traditional   17-19
declarative knowledge   23, 32
DENDRAL   85, 86, 87, 88, 91-92,
                                       137-151
– application   138-142
– generate-and-test   92, 137-138, 149
– Heuristic DENDRAL   139, 142-146

– knowledge elicitation	139-142
– META-DENDRAL	146-151
diagnosis	86, 94, 119, 120-121, 125-126, 130, 133-134
disease tree	122-127
domain dependence	31-33, 82, 85, 94, 99
EMYCIN	94
expert systems	
– classification	89-92
– developments	191-194
– principles	86-89
explanation facilities	87, 101, 102, 119, 129, 192, 193
failure-driven memory	193
5th Generation Computing	191
FORTRAN	134
frames	67-71, 174
– default value	69
– facet	69
– implementation in LISP	70
– inheritance hierarchy	68
– languages	71
– procedural attachment	69
– slot filler	68-69, 70
Fuzzy Set Theory	115
game tree	76, 79
generate-and-test	91-92, 137-138, 153, 154, 161
(*see also* control)	
geological models	104-107
(*see also* PROSPECTOR)	
GRAVIDA	94
GUIDON	101, 103, 119, 193
– tutorial rule	103

HEARSAY-II   194
heuristic   80-82, 92, 174-175
Heuristic DENDRAL   139, 142-146
  – evaluation   146
  – generator   144-145
  – planner   142-144
  – tester   145-146
HYDRO   94

inexact reasoning
  – CASNET   130, 133
  – INTERNIST   122, 123, 127-128
  – MYCIN   90-91, 96-97, 99
  – PROSPECTOR   104, 109-114
inference   33-34
  – bottom-up   78-79, 128, 134
  – inexact
      (see inexact reasoning)
  – logical   37-39, 43-49
  – rules of   45-49, 177
  – top-down   78-79, 128
INTERNIST   76, 91, 119-129
  – control   123, 125-128, 129
  – diagnostic strategy   120-121, 125-128
  – disease model   125, 127
  – evaluation   128-129
  – inexact inference   122, 123, 127-128
  – representation   121-125
is-a relation   61

judgemental reasoning
    (see inexact reasoning)

knowledge
  – associative   88
  – causal   88, 91
  – common sense   54
  – declarative   23, 32

- deep   191
- fact(s)   19-23, 28-29, 61
- procedural   23
- processing   18-19, 49-51
- rule(s)   19-23, 28-29
(*see also* representation)
knowledge-based approach   53-57, 85-89
knowledge elicitation   101-103, 139-142
KRL   71

least commitment   92, 167, 174, 176
LISP   51, 57-60, 61-62, 177, 191
logic
- argument   38, 39, 40, 41
- connectives   41, 43, 177-178
- content   38
- form   38, 45, 76
- inference   37-39, 43-49
- proof   47-49, 179-182, 182-187
- quantifiers   41-42, 178
(*see also* predicate calculus)
logic programming
(*see* PROLOG)

META-DENDRAL   146-151
- evaluation   151
- rule generation   149-151
MICRO-EXPERT   94
modus ponens   39, 45, 46, 48, 51
modus tollens   46, 47, 48
MOLGEN   71, 86, 92, 155, 161-179
- abstraction   92
- application   161-164
- constraints   164
- control   162-164, 174-175
- meta-planning   164
- planning strategy   164-171
- representation   171-174

MYCIN

	86, 90, 91, 93-103, 119, 121, 123, 142, 146, 193
– certainty factors	94, 95, 96-97
– context tree	98, 99
– control	95, 99
– evaluation	115-117
– explanation facility	101, 102-103
– inexact inference	90-91, 96-97, 99
– production system	93
– representation	94-96

ONCOCIN	101
OPS4/5	159, 160

PASCAL	24, 25, 26, 44
planning	86, 92, 162, 174-175
– meta-planning	164, 174
predicate calculus	39-51, 61, 177-182
– advantages	189-191
– automation	49-50, 51, 177-182
– clausal form	177, 178-179
– Horn clauses	183
– resolution theorem proving	177-182
(*see also* logic)	
probabilities	
(*see* inexact reasoning)	
problem-reduction	91
problem-solving	35, 53-57, 76, 85, 89-92, 115-117, 119-120, 137-138, 153-155, 177-178, 190-194
procedures	25-26
production systems	29-31, 39, 71-76
– backward-chaining	94, 95, 99
– control structure	71, 74-75, 115
– data-directed	94
– forward-chaining	95, 99
– goal-directed	94
– rules	71, 73, 144, 145

program-driven processing	27
PROLOG	51, 177, 182-189
– AND/OR tree	185, 186, 187
– backtracking	186, 187
– goal	185, 186, 187, 188
– Horn clauses	183
– subgoals	185
PROSPECTOR	86, 90, 91, 93, 103-115, 119, 193
– application	103-104
– control	107-109
– evaluation	115-117
– inexact reasoning	104, 107-114
– inference net	104-107
– production system	93
– semantic network	107
PUFF	94
R1	86, 92, 155-161
– abstraction	92, 153-155
– application	155
– control	155-157
– implementation	159-161
– knowledge-base	157-159
reasoning	
– common sense	49-50, 54
– inexact	34-35, 90, 93
– monotonic	50, 89, 189
– non-monotonic	50, 189
– problem reduction	91
recursion	20, 21
representation	17-33, 39-43, 53, 60-76
(*see also* frames, predicate calculus, production systems, semantic networks)	
resolution theorem proving	51, 177-182
– clausal form	178-179
– resolution procedure	179-182
rules	
(*see* knowledge *and* production system)	

SACOM 94
SAGE 94
script 71
search
– abstraction 92
– backtracking 23, 36, 56, 154, 156, 188
– breadth-first 22-23, 79
– data-directed 96
– depth-first 22-23, 79, 109, 185
– generate-and-test 91-92
– goal-directed 96
– heuristic 80-82, 92, 174-175
– least commitment 92, 167-171
– state-space 76-82, 89, 91-92
(*see also* control)
semantic networks 60-67
– case relations 66
– CASNET 91
– default values 66
– event representation 65-66
– implementation in LISP 61-62
– inheritance hierarchies 64
– is-a link 61, 63-64
– prototypes 65-67
– type/token distinction 63
SHRINK 193
Skolem function 178
SNOBOL 134
SPEX 176
state-space search 76-82, 89

TEIRESIAS 101-103, 119, 146
– meta-rules 102
– natural language facility 103
– rule model 102-103
theorem proving
(*see* resolution theorem proving)
top-down inference 78-79, 128
tree 22

– AND/OR	185, 186, 187
– context	98, 99
– decision	73
– disease	122-127
– game	76, 79
truth maintenance	189
uncertain evidence	90, 91
UNITS	71, 174
variables, representation of	20, 40
VM	94
well-formed formulas	45